# 2018 The MEGA Year

# 5778 The Year of the Open Door

DR. CAROLYN G. ANDERSON

2018 The MEGA Year

Book #2 of **#The7YearSeries**

Copyright © 2018 by Riley Press

All rights reserved. No part of this book may be reproduced or transmitted in any form or by any means, electronically or mechanically, including photocopying, recording, retrieval system, without prior written permission from the author, except for the inclusions of brief quotes in a review.

Published by Riley Press, a division of Integrity Productions & Promotions

Book Cover and Interior designed by Riley Press

Printed in the United States of America. All scripture quotations, unless otherwise indicated, are taken from the Holy Bible, New International Version®, NIV®. Copyright ©1973, 1978, 1984, 2011 by Biblica, Inc.TM Used by permission of Zondervan. All rights reserved worldwide. www.zondervan.com The "NIV" and "New International Version" are trademarks registered in the United States Patent and Trademark Office by Biblica, Inc.TM

Other scripture references are noted and were either taken from the MSG, KJV, NKJV or AMP versions of the Bible. Non-scripture references are also noted within the text and will not have its own reference page.

# Table of Contents

Dedication .................................................. 9
   Prophetic Testimonials ......................... 11
   Background ......................................... 13
Introduction – #MEGA Year ..................... 19
Purpose of the Book ................................. 27
Preface ..................................................... 33
Chapter 1 – Spin Cycle ............................. 39
   The Year 2016 ...................................... 40
Chapter 2 – The Year 2017 ...................... 47
Chapter 3 - The Year 5777 ....................... 53
Chapter 4 – New Leadership .................... 59
   Legal Authority ..................................... 59
   **The Remnants** .................................. 59
Chapter 5 – Who Am I? ........................... 67
Chapter 6 – Promises ............................... 75
   Seven Steps to Breakthrough ................ 77
   **Kingdom Building** ............................ 87
Chapter 7 – Rosh Hashanah ..................... 95
   Head of the Year ................................... 95
   **The Lord's Appointed Times** ........... 101
   **Times and Seasons** ......................... 104

**Numbers & Biblical Numerology** 110
Chapter 8 – The Year 5778 ...... 117
   **Ayin Chet** ...... 117
   The Year of the Open Door ...... 121
Chapter 9 – Happy New Year ...... 125
Chapter 10 – MEGA Year 2018 ...... 133
   **Making Everything Good Again** ...... 133
   **Light vs. Darkness** ...... 145
   **Number 8 (Infinity)** ...... 148
Chapter 11 - Palace Time ...... 155
   Wealth Transfer ...... 158
Chapter 12 – The Awakening ...... 165
Summary ...... 179
Confession ...... 194
78 Decrees & Declarations ...... 197
Personal Prayer ...... 205
Appreciation ...... 215
About the Author ...... 217
Connect with us! ...... 221
Other Books by Dr. Carolyn ...... 223

# **Dedication**

This book is dedicated to you and your Destiny!

# Prophetic Testimonials

When God's people need to hear a NOW word of the Lord, God sends Dr. Carolyn G. Anderson to let them know what He is saying for that season and time.

In 2017 The MVP Year, Dr. Carolyn brings forth the timing of the Lord when God will initiate 'the seven years of abundance as it was in the days of Joseph.

Dr. Carolyn is a Prophet who is compassionate, loving and anointed in this hour to bring forth the ministry of Royalty, Wealth and Health. This book is a must for those who have an ear to hear and an eye to see what the Spirit of the Lord is saying NOW!

**Apostle K. Anthony**
Kingdom Cathedral International Ministries

I established some grand goals for the beginning of 2016 so I was excited to petition heaven for manifestation. During the midpoint of 2016, I felt stuck. I decided to multi task by praying and doing my required work. I told God that I needed to hear a word from Him because I felt stuck.

When I got off work, I received a call from Prophet Carolyn telling me that she had a word for me. She shared a word that equipped and empowered me to move from feeling unstuck to ready to possess the land that God promised me. She is an on-time Prophet.

**Latreeta Burns**
Jericho Church Without Walls

# Background

## HAPPY 2018

The Prophetic calling on Dr. Carolyn's life can be traced back to her childhood. She was very discerning and oftentimes would know something was going to happen before it did. She would choose her friends wisely because God revealed the intentions of their hearts towards her and therefore she knew the right friends to hang around.

Subsequently, she made very wise choices because she could envision the results. There are very specific moments where Dr. Carolyn recalls making decrees (back then she just spoke not realizing what she was doing), about things to come in her life. There's one very specific moment in high school, where she told one of her best friends that Kevel (husband now) would be her husband within 10 years. She wasn't interested in him at that time not even as a boyfriend. It would so happen that ten years later, Kevel became her husband and still is to this day. There are numerous accounts where she would know specific dates and times of events including the birthdates of her children, prior to the occasion.

The prophetic calling on her life truly gave birth on 3.1.03, where she had an encounter with God and He blessed her with the gift of speaking in tongues and the prophetic anointing. It was from that moment that she would begin to flourish and realize that God speaks to her in various ways, especially through the alpha-numeric language, nature, and blessed her with the gift to understand times and seasons. She also has the gift of understanding the steps to wealth, healing and being very strategic.

To thresh the gift, she and her husband were both ordained as Apostles and Prophets and lead a Global Ministry that's transforming lives.

Most recently, God has given Dr. Carolyn very specific dates and times for the body so that they can understand His plans and purposes for their lives. Allow the message within this text to speak to you so that you can participate in God's timing and season.

The **TIME IS NOW!** It is the appointed time to begin your new journey and start fresh. Therefore, meet the **Fresh Voice** that God is using for such a time as this.

*"There is a time for everything, and a season for every activity under the heavens:"*

***Ecc 3:1 NIV***

**Pause Moment……….**

Take a few minutes and just begin to write what you are hearing in your spirit. What are your desires? What would you like to see happen for you in 2018? What are your Goals, Dreams and Aspirations? Just take this moment to pause, reflect on your life and write.

_____

_____

_____

_____

_____

_____

_____

_____

_____

# Introduction – #MEGA Year

Welcome to the #**MEGA** Year, when God is **M**aking **E**verything **G**ood **A**gain as it was in the beginning. According to **Genesis 1:8,** it states that ***"...And God saw that it was good."*** Everything that God made in the beginning was good and as we embrace this good year, get ready to experience some new beginnings as He's making all things **new** and **good** again.

*"...And God saw that it was good:"*

***Gen 1:18 NIV***

For the past 15 years, I have been seeking God prior to the beginning of each new year for a theme or scripture for my immediate family for that year! He's given a word each time for the year. That word would carry us consistently throughout the year and it would become the bedrock on which we stand. What I mean by that is, whenever something arose that seemed contrary to the word that the Lord had given us, we would declare what God said about that particular year. This is how we were able to fight and combat what was happening in our lives. It also allowed us to live in peace and harmony throughout the year, because we knew that no matter what happened, it would turn out for our good, because God had given us a word for the year.

When my husband and I started Pastoring in 2011, we sought the Lord even further for a theme for the ministry. In addition to the general word for the church, each member received personal prophetic ministry. Consequently, we also started learning more about our Jewish roots and about God's biblical calendar, which is different from the Gregorian/Julius calendar that the western world is more familiar with. Nevertheless, with the new knowledge of God's biblical calendar, we started living according to both calendars, except our celebrations, observations, feasts and times of fasting are according to the Jewish/Hebraic calendar.

During very specific appointed times with God, He revealed to me that He elevated me from being just a Prophet that minister's personal prophecies, to a Prophet on a Global basis that understands His timing and seasons and was a strategic voice that transform lives. From then leading up to today, I have been declaring the meaning of the YEARS and what God has in store for His people. It's time to position yourself in the receiving mode and welcome **2018** with excitement. It's your **#MEGA** Year! It's time to do things **BIG**, because we serve a Great **BIG,** Mighty and Powerful God.

Has God given you a specific word or scripture for your 2018? If so write it below. If you're not sure, you can <u>fast and pray</u> and ask God if He has a specific word or scripture for you. If He hasn't, no big deal, because whether God has given you a specific word or not, He is giving you one NOW and letting you know that this is your MEGA Year, your new beginnings, and your year of a **good** life! The #**MEGA** Year is your year and it's your season to prosper and experience the abundance.

**NOTES..........**

_____

_____

Not all the time God gives a specific word to everyone that's separate from the Global word that He has declared for that year. His specific word can be embedded within the overarching word, such as the **MEGA** theme for **2018** that I will share more about in the text. For example, in **2017**, the Major theme for the year was that it was the **MVP YEAR** and **MVP** stood for (**Manifestations, Victo-ries (the Re's), Purposes established and Promises fulfilled**). This was the title of the first book that I wrote that's a part of the 7-year series.

You can purchase the book here: Https://www.amazon.com/author/carolynganderson

While part of the theme was about Victories, a subset within that was that it was also the year of the **Re's**. The first **re** was a **RE-SET**. In the book **2017 The MVP Year**, I wrote 57 Re's that could be applied to individual lives. Many experienced re-plevin, re-marriages, restitution, re-location, re-lationships restored and so on. For me personally, I knew that God was resetting some things in my life and redeeming my time. I also know that I would experience many manifestations in my life which I did.

Therefore, the specific word or theme for my life that God shared with me was a part of the overall word of the **Lord for 2017**. Even if He gives you a specific scripture or word, knowing God's divine nature, I am sure it fits within the context of being a **MEGA Year**, a year of a good life, a year of complete new beginnings and a year when you shall experience a turnaround.

**Trust God!** He's getting ready to make things new in your life. I believe that you're about to have one of the best years of your life and experience some **MEGA** things in **this year**.

## Purpose of the Book

This book is the second of seven books that's a part of the Prophetic Series called **#The7Year.** The purpose of the book is to share what God is doing right **NOW** and what's to come. It's time for the people of God to participate in God's timing so that **His will** be done on earth as it is in Heaven.

God has revealed part of His Sovereign plan and I am so excited to share it with you. You are about to experience some new and refreshing things and I believe that it will be a **good** year for you. According to Amos 3:7 NIV it says, <u>*"Surely the Sovereign Lord does nothing without revealing his plan to his servants the Prophets."*</u> Well, God has revealed some amazing things, so let the revelations flow to you as you read this book.

God has a set time for everything and He desires for His people to be in sync with His timing so that we can truly live out our purpose and kingdom mandate. Don't you want to hear "well done, my good and faithful servant?" I know I do. I have purposed in my heart that I will get to heaven empty, meaning that I would have used every gift He has given me, lived life fully and maximized my purpose and full potential.

Subsequently, the purpose of the book is to be a voice for God and to share elements of His timing, strategies on how to effectively activate your purpose and how to walk with God. Life is easier and more peaceful when one understands God's timing. It also makes you wiser and makes the journey of life more pleasant and harmonious.

According to Psalm 90:12 NIV, it says ***"Teach us to number our days, that we may gain a heart of wisdom"*** and Job 14:5 NIV says ***"A person's days are determined; you have decreed the number of his months and have set limits he cannot exceed."*** Thus, knowing what season of life you are in and where you are going plays an intricate role in your destiny.

According to Ecclesiastes 3:1-8 NIV ***"There is a time for everything, and a season for every activity under the heavens: a time to be born and a time to die, a time to plant and a time to uproot, a time to kill and a time to heal, a time to tear down and a time to build, a time to weep and a time to laugh, a time to mourn and a time to dance, a time to scatter stones and a time to gather them, a time to embrace and a time to refrain from embracing, a time to search and a time to give up, a time to keep and a time to throw away, a time to tear and a time to mend, a time*** *to be silent and a time to speak, a time to love and a time to hate, a time for war and a time for peace."*

Now is the time to experience the **MEGA LiFE**™, it's time for a fresh start, a new beginning. It's time to make millions, to live in excess, always having more than enough. It's time for the Great Abundance as it was in the beginning! So, get ready for the **#MEGA LiFE**™ because it belongs to you.

NOTES..........

_____

_____

_____

_____

_____

_____

# Preface

Before going forward and sharing the good things about the year **5778/2018**, let's first do a quick recap so that there's a better understanding and a more in-depth perspective as to why God is **Making Everything Good Again.**

The year **2015** and **2016** were years when God had to do a pause and shift some things around. He had to do this because there were some that were declaring that destruction was forthcoming. Yet, myself and a few other Prophets were not sensing that's what God was doing. God was sharing that there's a great abundance coming, and while there's a great abundance coming, it would include some tests. All major elevations require moments of testing.

I believe that it was this foreshadowing of the tests that were being perceived as destruction and judgement. Prophets are able to foresee certain things and at times when it's not clear, they will sometimes lean more towards God sending judgement. It's not a bad thing, as one of the appointed roles of a Prophet is to rebuke and correct considering that God always sends warming before judgement. Since Prophets are to subject themselves one to another, I did just that. I laid low per se and just listened to what they were saying, until I had further clarification from God.

The enemy is very cunning and I have come to know some of his tactics and it would NOT have been a good thing for Prophets to be arguing and debating against each other publicly, as that would create confusion and doubt and that's exactly what the enemy wanted.

It turns out that God was doing a major shifting and transition, such as the changing of guards and handing the baton to a new set of leaders who He was getting ready to use for such a time as this. These leaders, such as myself have been laying low in deep communion with God, hearing His new strategies and downloads. This is exactly what a RESET is. God is such a gentleman and very respectful and therefore He does not speak in the noise. He speaks only when you have the time to truly hear what He has to say and oftentimes that requires moments of extended consecration and alone time with God.

Therefore, the years 2015 and 2016 were years that were pause moments, resets, reshuffling, and testing. While there were many ups and downs, trials and tribulations and some victories, what God was doing was necessary to get us to where we are today and for the years to come. They were preparation years for the Great

Abundance as it was in the days of Joseph the Dreamer. Many had experienced the Pit Season, Potiphar's House Season, Prison Season and was patiently awaiting the **Palace** Season, <u>**but first**</u> God had to squeeze some heaviness out of His people to change clothes for the **Palace** Season.

**Moments of Reflection......................**

Pause and take a moment and reflect back on the year 2015 and write down what you can remember about that year.

_____

_____

_____

_____

_____

## Chapter 1 – Spin Cycle

Life is a journey and not a final destination and on that journey, there are seasons and cycles that exist. The seasons are a compilation of different processes and sometimes one season can be longer than the other. One of my favorite character in the bible is Joseph the Dreamer and he went through several seasons that led to cycles in his life. One of the most fascinating moments that's described in the bible is that **before** Joseph entered one of this last season (the Palace), the bible said, he changed his clothes. *"So Pharaoh sent for Joseph, and he was quickly brought from the dungeon. When he had shaved and changed his clothes, he came before Pharaoh." Genesis 41:14 NIV*

Why would God use a metaphor of changing **clothes** as an expression for Joseph leaving his prison season to get to the palace season? God could have used anything, but he chose clothes. There are many explanations, such as, clothes being a covering and how at times, one needs to change his or her alignment and affiliation. In this case, God's expression of clothing represents one of the processes of life. He uses this analogy as one of the ways to get us to understand times and seasons in its simplest form. It was the perfect example to describe the years 2016 and leading up to 2017 and now 2018.

## The Year 2016

The year **2016** was like a Spin Cycle that occurs during the process of doing laundry. It was a year that had many ups and downs, trials and tribulations, some victories, and a feeling that words couldn't describe. There were many Christians that lost hope and some came to the verge of totally giving up. Perhaps you were one of them that felt like 2016 was a world-wind year. That's even if you remember the year or perhaps it was so bad that you have chosen to let it go. Or, it's possible that it was an okay year. One minute when it seems like things were going great, suddenly it was disappointment and brokenness. Just when things seemed hopeful, it was deferred. Some people literally became physically ill, while waiting for a change.

Just like doing a load of laundry, there's a process that must take place to get to the finished product. There's a process to get the clothes clean and ready to wear again, which represents the changing of seasons. This process of getting dirty laundry to clean clothes cannot be accomplished with just one equipment. It requires two equipment's, a washer and a dryer. God is saying that to succeed in this next seven years of abundance that's at hand, it will require divine alignments, strategic collaborations, unity and togetherness to thrive and be victorious.

Like any process there are steps that are necessary to have a quality product or result. The laundry process is a four-step process. First the clothes are washed, rinsed, then the spin cycle, then dried. The spin cycle is the step before putting the clothes in the dryer. If the clothes are not **removed** after the spin cycle and placed in the dryer, they will begin to smell.

When doing laundry, there are different options to choose from for when washing and drying. Depending on the type and color of the garments, the cycle can either be hot, cold, warm or a combination of both. Not all cycles will be the same. The same is true for going through tests. They don't all look alike. For me personally, I knew that God was healing my emotional ups and downs and some traumatic situations that entered my life during the earlier stage of my marriage.

The spin cycle in **2016** was necessary as it was meant to squeeze out the last ounce of heaviness so that we could enter the new finishing cycle of 2017 and step out in the **MEGA** cycle of 2018. God had to heal some wounds, some deep soul wounds, emotional and relational issues, brokenness, financial drought and some heavy burdens that His people were carrying. The clothes needed to be changed and those that were pressed needed to so that they met the pre-requisite to enter the Palace Season and walk in complete abundance. This was a set-up and a precursor for the reset, manifestations and victories of **2017**.

**Moments of Reflection......................**

Pause and take a moment and reflect back on the year **2016** and write down what you can remember. Did you go through any tests or trials? Did you experience any healing during **2016**? Do you know what God had to squeeze out of you, if anything?

_____

_____

_____

_____

_____

_____

_____

## Chapter 2 – The Year 2017

### Seventeen – the number of Victory

The year **2017** was the year of the **MVP** (Manifestations, Victo-ries, Purpose and Promises being established). It was the year for healing and being in good health and it was God's **RESET year.** It was a year of preparation for the **SEVEN YEAR CYCLE** as it was in the days of Joseph the dreamer, starting with the seven years of Abundance as written in Genesis 41:29 NIV *"Seven years of great abundance are coming..."*

The number seventeen (17) has been associated with VICTORY. Before I did the research on the number 17, God revealed to me that 2017 was the year of many **VICTO-RIES and the (Re's),** such as re-set, re-demption, re-velation, re-newal, re-stitution and so on. He said many victories will **MANIFEST** in 2017. Many had suffered in 2016 and so 2017 was the comeback year. Part of this GREAT VICTORY was the mass healing that took place in many people's life. I wrote about this healing in my #1 Best Selling Book, **Heal-thy LiFE - Heal-thy Land**, where I expressed that the first place that the word healing appears in the bible is Genesis 20:17. This wasn't a coincidence. God knew that before the foundations of the world that 2017 would start the healing ministry all over again. Many had not experienced healing for whatever reason, but God wanted His people to know that they don't need to look for a cure or accept bad news, because He sent His Good News to heal every disease and to set us free.

In the Bible the number 17 symbolizes "overcoming the enemy" and "complete victory." God overcame the sins of rebellious humans when he flood the earth through rain on the 17th of the second Hebrew month. Noah's ark and its eight passengers rested on the mountains of Ararat on the 17th of the seventh month (right in the middle of God's annual Holy period known as the Feast of Tabernacles).

Jesus Christ gained a complete victory over death and the grave when God resurrected him near sunset on Nisan 17 (Saturday, April 8, 30 A.D.) (This paragraph taken from biblestudy.org)

In the year 2017 God renewed His Covenant with you as He declared in Genesis 17:1-17. Whether you knew it or not, you got to participate in His covenant because it was a promise given to Abraham and his descendants. Whether you are a Jew or a Christian you are part of the covenant because you are one of Abraham's descendants. You are a part of God's Royal family. *"When Abram was ninety-nine years old, the Lord appeared to him and said, "I am God Almighty; walk before me faithfully and be blameless. Then I will make my covenant between me and you and will greatly increase your numbers." Abram fell facedown, and God said to him, "As for me, this is my covenant with you: You will be the father of many nations. No longer will you be called Abram; your name will be Abraham, for I have made you a father of many nations. I will make you very fruitful; I will make nations of you, and kings will come from you. I will establish my covenant as an everlasting covenant between me and you and your descendants after you for the generations to come, to be your God and the God of your descendants after you."*

Abraham didn't know how God was going to fulfill the promises. He didn't know the process. He just believed that if God spoke something then it's true. God has spoken that you have a victorious life and therefore it's up to you to believe it, own it and start taking the necessary steps toward your destiny. You have a **MEGA LiFE**™ at hand.

**Moments of Reflection.......................**

Take a moment and pause and reflect on the year 2017. Did you experience any victories or Re's? Perhaps healing? Take a moment and write about your 2017.

_____

_____

_____

_____

_____

_____

_____

_____

_____

## Chapter 3 - The Year 5777

Earlier in the Introduction, I shared about God's **Biblical calendar** and the Gregorian calendar, which is the one you're probably more familiar with. God established His biblical calendar so that the Children of Israel would remember Him and set aside certain times as appointed times with Him. While we are no longer operating under the law of Moses, God's biblical calendar still exists.

There are certain set times that are days of observance and is also believed to be days that God does mass healing, blessings, forgiveness, and review the book of life. One of those appointed times is **Rosh Hashanah** (usually around September or October) and **Yom Kippur** also known as The Day of Atonement. Rosh Hashanah is considered the Head of the Year or the Civilian New Year. It is believed to be the time that God made civilization (Adam and Eve).

Therefore, every year around this time, the Jewish people and other Kingdom followers will observe this day and the 10 days of awe (Yom Kippur) thereafter. Yom Kippur is one of God's High Holy Days and is said to be the day that God forgives our sins and re-start our lives with His blessings.

Our immediate family celebrates Rosh Hashanah, Yom Kippur and the other appointed days to honor God and to show Him that we believe His Word and are participating with His time and season. We have seen tremendous blessings in our lives, since wholeheartedly following the Hebraic Calendar, including honoring the Sabbath Day as a holy day and a day of rest.

On October 2, 2016, it was Rosh Hashanah, the New Year 5777. The year 5777 was the year of the **Triple Crown**, the year of God

**perfecting some things in His people.** It was the year of completion, resets, and the year of **divine rest**. This is not a rest where you do nothing, but rather rest from the enemy and the celebration of Victories.

If you follow God's calendar and the Gregorian calendar, you get to enjoy and celebrate three (3) New Year which are: (1) Rosh Hashanah, (2) January 1$^{st}$ and (3) Nisan (around March-April), which is the Biblical New Year- the time when the children of Israel had the Great Exodus from Egypt. The Jewish people celebrate this time also as a re-start of God's calendar. You see, God loves celebration and He loves to give opportunities to start over, to renew and fresh new beginnings.

Therefore 5777/2017 was a great year in the lives of God's people and it was the perfect year for God to assign new leaders, to complete the Spin Cycle, to demonstrate manifestations as a way of preparation for the seven years of Abundance that's at hand. He is truly a great father and I hope that you are ready to experience the #**MEGA** Year. It shall be great indeed.

 **Moment……………….**

What are your Aha moments from this section? What revelation/s did you receive? Did you learn anything new that you didn't know before?

_____

_____

_____

_____

_____

# Chapter 4 – New Leadership

## Legal Authority

The experiences in the previous years were all a set up by God to see who were strong enough to withstand the storms and pass the test as the pre-qualifications for promotions in the Kingdom of God. In every era, whether it's the biblical days or today, at certain timeframes God will change guards and appoint new leaders in position to carry on the race. The baton has to be passed from one player to the next, so that the team can win the race. If it's not passed, then the race does not continue.

## The Remnants

God has raised up a generation that He's calling the **NOW GENERATION**. These are those in their 20's, 30's, 40's, 50's and some 60's and 70's that have not gotten their opportunity to lead and will now get that opportunity. He's raising up a new set of leaders and warriors to carry the baton as the race continues to the finish line. There's one particular generation that God is distinctly using as the Leaders for today and that's the Generation X. Gen X are those born between 1965 to 1976 – and in 2018 are ages 42-53. Out of all the generations, they have the shortest range in years, with only 11 years. All other generations age ranges are 18 to 21 years. For example, Gen Y, affectionately known as the Millennials, were born between 1977 to 1995 and today are ages 23-41 with a range of 18 years.

God revealed that Gen X have been x'ed out and passed over for years. There are so many conferences and resources for Millennials and oftentimes no mention of any other age group. Typically, the Baby Boobers (born between 1946-1964) will mentor and train the Millennials but forget about Gen X. God said Gen-X have been the silent generation, the un-mentored, the cast outs and the forgotten, but He has not forgotten them. God will never allow His order to be out of place and so Generation X cannot be left out and passed over anymore and God himself says He has given the baton to them to lead and to train others.

As we embrace the #**MEGA** Year, God is also doing some age reversals, renewals and resets and so the 42's will now feel and look like the 24-year-old and so on. There will be a change from the Moses' to the Joshua's. From the Elijah's to the Elisha's and from the Naomi's to the Ruth's. These new leaders are the Re-mnants. God is raising up a Joshua generation with the Key of David, with the Joseph's Anointing and the spirit of Deborah to fulfill all of God's prophetic promises to Israel and His Beloved Church. While God is releasing the **FRESH VOICES** (*the Joshua's, Joseph's,*

*Ester's, Deborah's to birth forth something new;* He still need the Paul's, Elisha's, Peter's and so on, to be mentors and guides as they impart their wisdom and lead authentically.

## **Don't Hold on to the Baton**

Sometimes those that have labored for years, can get envious when a new kid comes on the block per se. However, God is saying, oh I have not forgotten anyone. He's using the Elijah's to build up the Elisha's and the reward is GREAT. All will inherit and receive his or her reward.

## **You're Chosen**

I believe that you are reading this book not by coincidence or accident, but by divine appointment. It doesn't matter what age group or generation you fall within, you are part of God's **MEGA YEAR** and **MEGA PLAN**. I believe that God wants you to know that it's time for you to truly walk in your authentic purpose and be a leader in your own sphere of influence. Do you know what you were called to be and to do? Are you crystal clear on your authentic purpose?

## It's Your Time

You had to go through the pain, trials, tribulations and sufferings in the past, because pain precedes purpose. It wasn't until Joseph the Dreamer went through his moments of pain, that he truly gave birth to his purpose. You had to experience the contractions and the birthing pains. It was designed by God to give you authority and influence in that area of your life. You can't have an anointing or authority in any area of life unless you've first walked through it. For you to be victorious in anything and to have legal authority you must first experience it, be tested in it so that you can have dominion over it.

To have wealth you must first know what it's like to be broke. To have authority in healing you must first be healed, which means that you had to be sick in some area of your life (financial, health, business etc.,) so that you have the anointing in that area to help others overcome. Jesus had to go through the test and trials and even death to win. He experienced temptation from the enemy. He experienced persecution. He paid the price and it was after the test, the spin cycle, that God granted Him the reward and gave Him the church as His bride. It was all a part of God's divine plan.

So, if you look at your life, the problems and heartaches that you have experienced and walked through, just know that it was God's way of granting you legal permission and authority over that area and now you can help someone else and build up the Kingdom of God. You've probably been broken enough for two or three people and are ready for the change. Your patience was a blessing so congratulations. It's time to walk in your **#MEGA YEAR**. According to James 1:12 AMP, it says *"Blessed (happy, to be envied) is the man who is patient under trial and stands up under temptation, for when he has stood the test and been approved, he will receive the victor's crown of life which God has promised to those who love Him."* Get your clothes ready, it's time to step into your royal season and wear that golden crown.

**Moments of Reflection..................**

Do you believe that you were called to lead?

_____

_____

_____

_____

# Chapter 5 – Who Am I?

*"The greatest tragedy in life is not death, but it's life without meaning, without a purpose"*
**Dr. Myles Munroe**

The Year 2018 is truly the Year to know without the shadow of a doubt what your purpose in life is. In order to have the **MEGA LiFE**™ and enjoy the fullness of the prophetic decree for 2018, you must truly walk in your authentic **PURPOSE**. This is not the year to be a replicable of somebody else or a carbon copy of another person or to live out someone else's vision. This is your time and your season.

You've probably heard this before and it's very likely that because your life has been so difficult that you don't believe it's your time or your season to shine. It is possible though, that you may have hoped and believed that it was your time, but you weren't truly living, breathing and being the authentic you. Oftentimes, this is what I have observed in my Clients, Coachee's and students that I train and teach about Purpose.

This season, you will need to truly know your purpose in life and live that life fully every day. This is a huge part of living in the **2018 MEGA** Year. The late Dr. Myles Munroe said**, "The greatest tragedy in life is not death, but life without meaning, without a purpose."** Therefore, it's time to truly live life with meaning. It's important to know where you fit in, within the seven spheres of influence, also referred to as the seven mountains and actually I have added three more areas to the existing seven. What area/s of influence do you believe that you are called to? Do your gifts shine in **Business, Media, Family, Arts & Entertainment, Ministry, Government and/or Education?** Perhaps it's in **Healthcare, Finance** or **Technology? (my added three).**

Sometimes you are called to more than one area and you may even find yourself being able to navigate in all the areas, but knowing at least which sphere of influence (mountain) is your primary one will make life easier and more peaceful. Oftentimes when one is not sure of who he or she was born to be and do, then he or she will find his or herself confused and not clear about the direction they should go. This will cause frustration, burnout or a sense of being overwhelmed and all this leads to an unhealthy life.

Dr. Myles Munroe (1992) also said **"fulfillment in life is dependent on becoming and doing what one was born to be and do. Anything less makes life an enemy and death a friend**." It is essential, vital, crucial and necessary that there's understanding of the fundamental principle of purpose and pursue it wholeheartedly. For without purpose, life has no direction and those who don't know where they are going will probably end up somewhere else. It's my desire and more importantly, God's desire that you live the **#MEGA LiFE™** because He's making everything good in your life again.

Don't end up being one that dies, never truly living his or her purpose. There are several graves with unfulfilled potential just lying dead. They died full, and not empty. I want to die empty, meaning that if I should go to heaven before Christ return that I want to have used every gift, talent, and ability that was given to me to the fullest potential.

You are alive for such a time as this, so activate your PURPOSE and walk it out. Ask God what is your purpose in life? He will answer you. If you need guidance to get started on understanding your purpose, you can find resources on my website at www.carolynganderson.com.

There are still **PROMISES** in your life yet to be fulfilled and that's a good thing. Bishop Bill Hamon (one of my spiritual father) said that he once knew a man that told him that all his **promises** and prophetic words came to past and that man died shortly after. The point is, it's good to continue to receive prophetic words and to have **promises** yet to be fulfilled, that way you always have something to look forward to. If you just open one of the books that is found in the blueprint for life (The Bible), you will see that God has **promised** you a good and a great life. Start decreeing that you are walking in your season of the **MEGA LiFE**™ and don't stop decreeing it.

The enemy will lie and whisper deceptive words. He will bring up your past or even remind you of the Spin Cycle year, but just remember that those years were necessary. They were a part of the **process** of getting to the **Palace Season** of your life and now you are an overcomer. You have passed the test and you can enjoy the abundance that's at hand and forthcoming. It's time for a new beginning and your **MEGA LiFE™**. I pray that your **5778/2018** year will be one of the best year ever!

**Now it's time for a Pause Moment. Take some time and jot down what you believe your Purpose in life is. If you know your Purpose Statement or Vision Statement, write it down as well. Finally write down which of the seven (7) or (9) areas of influence you believe that you are called to.**

NOTES..........

_____

_____

_____

_____

_____

# Chapter 6 – Promises

**Time to Step Forth**

**Activate your Promises**

Life is a Journey and a journey requires a process to get to the destination. God could have birth Christ as a full-grown man, like he did with Adam, but He didn't do that. God allowed Jesus to go through a process to birth forth the promise of re-demption. While God's PROMISES are sure, the process is something He normally does not share. The process is based on the decisions and choices that you make daily. God promised me that I would be the mother of three and that one of the three would be a son. What He didn't tell me was that I would have to go through a fight to birth forth that son. My son was declared dead in my womb. I was hospitalized for weeks. One night, the resident doctor on duty decided that he was going to abort the baby because he thought that there was no life in my womb. It was a good thing that I was familiar with healthcare and knew that I could refuse care. I did that, because while I couldn't feel my son in my womb, I knew by faith that He was alive.

Today this son is eight (8) years old. I had to go through a process to birth forth the promise. God used the process that I went through to help so many other families that had difficulty conceiving, going through losses or simply just giving birth to believe again. Through this process, I birth forth and published a book titled, **"Pregnant with a Promise"** that is in high-demand. The book goes into details about losses, and births and what to do when it seems like your dream has died. Do the dreams live again? Yes, they do! Stand on the word of God, believe by

Faith and do the works that's necessary to see your promises manifest. You will need to fight for your prophetic promises. Do not let the enemy win. You already have the VICTORY! Your process could end up being a book, TV Show, Ministry, Conference or a Testimony that's designed to be a blessing to you and to others. I decree and declare that your promises and purpose will not die, but will live. Take the necessary steps to not just survive but to thrive and experience your **BREAKTHROUGH**, because your **MEGA Year** is at hand.

## Seven Steps to Breakthrough

A person experiences the most pain and brokenness right before breakthrough. In the bible, right before Jesus was getting ready to REDEEM us, to set the captives free, to die for us, the pain and pressure intensified. In fact, he travailed and asked God to remove the cup from Him. He asked his buddies to pray with him, but they fell asleep.

I know at times you may feel alone like there's no one to pray with you or like no one understands what you are going through. That's not the case. Even if no human being understands your situation, Jesus does. I decree and declare that God will release angels on your behalf right now to minister to you and to help you through this season and time if it's a difficult one.

Jesus is the best example of the steps that are needed for breakthrough. In the book of Luke when Jesus was ministering to the multitudes there came a point when they all got hungry and needed to eat. The disciples told Jesus to send the people away so that they can go and eat and find a place to stay. Jesus in-turn would demonstrate the seven steps to receive a breakthrough and showed how we all have authority for breakthrough if we follow these simple steps. Why do you need a breakthrough? Being able to break through the ups and downs of life is necessary for the **MEGA Year**. This is the season why God is stabilizing the lives of His people and separating light from darkness. A sign of the **light** on your life will be evident when you are living in the abundance.

The text reads, Luke 9:10-17 NIV **"*When the apostles returned, they reported to Jesus what they had done. Then he took them with him and they withdrew by themselves to a town called Bethsaida, but the crowds learned about it and followed him. He welcomed them and spoke to them about the kingdom of God, and healed those who needed healing. Crowds followed him and he spoke about the Kingdom of God and those that needed to be healed were healed. Late in the afternoon the Twelve came to him*** *and said, "Send the crowd away so they can go to the surrounding villages and countryside and find food and lodging, because we are in a remote place here." He replied, "You give them something to eat." They answered, "We have only five loaves of bread and two fish---unless we go and buy food for all this crowd." (About five thousand men were there.) But he said to his disciples, "Have them sit down in groups of about fifty each." The disciples did so, and everyone sat down. Taking the five loaves and the two fish and looking up to heaven, he gave thanks and broke them. Then he gave them to the disciples to distribute to the people. They all ate and were satisfied, and the disciples picked up twelve basketfuls of broken pieces that were left over.*

### Luke 9: 11-17

**The Steps are:**

1.  **SPOKE** (Decree & Declaration) Luke 9:13 NIV He replied, *"You give them something to eat." They answered, "We have only five loaves of bread and two fish---unless we go and buy food for all this crowd."* (Use what you have)

2.  **STRATEGY** - Luke 9:14 NIV (About five thousand men were there.) But he said to his disciples, *"Have them sit down in groups of about fifty each."*

It's time to get a STRATEGY because it's BREAKTHROUGH time. Having a Strategy is so critical. Can you imagine the chaos it would have been if Jesus did not have a Strategy? If the multitudes were not sitting in groups of 50, it would be disastrous to feed everyone without them bombarding Jesus and the disciples.

3.     **ACTIVATION** - Luke 9:16 NIV *Taking the five loaves and the two fish* (7 Tools) 7 WORDS, 7 years of blessings, 7 streams of income, 7 mountains come down. 5000 People!

4.     **APPEAL TO HEAVEN** Luke 9:16 *and looking up to heaven...* (John Henderson has a great book on this)

5.     **GAVE THANKS** Luke 9:16

6.     **BROKE THEM** (Luke 9:16 (must be broken before you experience a breakthrough) spirit of Multiplication (COMMUNION) - Unity in GOD!

Some of you are in Step 6 right now, waiting and ready to eat with LEFTOVERS. You've been broken, felt somewhat hopeless, can feel the wind of change coming, anticipating the great and mighty move of God, BUT WONDERING WHEN WILL IT HAPPEN.

Some of you are in the broken stages right now and are about to EAT and eat good with leftovers - 12 basketful.

7. **THEY ALL ATE** / Luke 9:17 It's time to EAT in your MEGA Year and walk in the abundant blessings. During Joseph's 7 years of abundance, what did they do? They all had something to eat, right? Joseph had a plan, God gave him the solution to the problem. He gave him a Strategy. Joseph was a Strategist which made him a Solutionist all because he walked in his purpose.

### Activate your BREAKTHROUGH

Right before a baby is born as its coming through the birth canal it's not getting any air, thus, it's not breathing. You may feel like you're not getting any air, like you're suffocating, but God wants you to know that suddenly, your head will push through and you will birth forth the new you. It's time to cut the umbilical cord and eat. Get your **Strategy** in place.

As an Executive Vice President for a Firm, I go into organizations, corporations, churches etc., and review, implement or coach them through their strategic plans. It's the #1 selling product and service in the business. It's a strategic plan that companies like Starbucks, Apple and others use to get them from a thousandaire company to millionaire, to billionaire and now heading to trillionaire. There are churches today that have a great vision and awaiting the promises of God but do not have a Strategy. Some organizations have a strategy but do not know how to execute it. There are families with no Strategy and no sense of direction.

There's an interesting story in Luke 16 about a man that used wisdom and implemented a strategy. This person was messing up and about to lose his job. When he realized it, he started to think of a Strategy that will change the situation. He figured out a plan and it went well.

What's surprising though is what Jesus said in the story. He said that **those in the world are wiser and take care of their own versus Christians**. This is very sad, yet true, however since God is making all things new again, let's hope that Christians will become wise and collaborate to rebuild the kingdom.

It's appears that Christian's are the only organized group of people that don't seem to work together to build up the kingdom of God. Why is that? Most Christians seem to be okay with the status quo of life, but GOD SEES STATUS QUO AS LUKEWARM and HE SPREWS it OUT. YOU shouldn't desire to be the worker bee that is happy with just getting a paycheck, and able to afford the cellular phone bill and catch a movie, and consider life to be good. That's not Kingdom living and that's not a **GOOD LiFE**™. When God made everything, He said it was good and He gave mankind everything that's needed to multiply and have dominion. What happened to being the head and not the tail? What about running the business and not working for others? What about owning the credit unions and the bank? What about living that Royal Kingdom LiFE?

It's time to get a STRATEGY that works. It's time to get a Strategic Vision Map™ and get your life, business and/or ministry in order. It's time to experience the **MEGA LiFE™**. Let's participate in this new era, the new time and walk in the abundance and the overflow. The Strategy I mentioned above can be found here: http://www.carolynganderson.com/coaching.*html*.

The law of promotion can only be activated when you have a strategy. Joseph was promoted to His Purpose and his life of abundance, when He executed his Strategy. God trusted Joseph and he knew that no matter what He gave Joseph that he would make good use of it. No matter what season or situation in Joseph's life, he made good use of his time and his attitude was always strategic. Can God trust you with what He has given you? God loves everyone, but He doesn't trust everyone.

Trust is earned by following and doing what you set yourself out to do without wavering. In the past, I used to wonder why God keeps giving me more and more stuff to do, or more and more prophecies to share. I stopped wondering and simply asked God, why do you give me so much responsibility, revelations, insights and messages? His answer was quick and to the point. He said, **"I trust you."** He said that no matter what He gives me to do, I find a way to do it and that I cared about pleasing Him more than pleasing myself. Now I ask God for the grace to carry out the missions and work that He gives to me and so should you. If you are already doing that and God trusts you, congratulations!!!

God wants you to take some time and begin to implement, review or re-vise your strategy and make things happen. The past years have been so difficult that many questioned their significance in life because of what they went through. They didn't see themselves as being of any value and some even thought of taking their own lives. If you were one of those, well thank God that you are here, because you have a great **BIG** life to live and it's time to build the Kingdom and inherit your sphere of influence. You are NOT a mistake because you were born for such a time as this. Let the year **5778/2018** be your new beginning.

## **Kingdom Building**

In 2 Samuel, chapter 6 it talks about the story of David when he was bringing the Ark of the Covenant back to Jerusalem. David's purpose was to place the **Ark of the Covenant** on his **shoulders** in transport back to the city. Instead, David placed it on a cart that was in front of him, while he followed behind the people that were with him. The Ark was about to fall and one of David's servant Uzzah, reached out and grabbed it, so that it wouldn't touch the ground, considering that it's very sacred. God struck Uzzah dead, because while he was doing a good deed, it wasn't his purpose to first be leading the path of the **Ark of the Covenant** and second to touch it. David was angry and perplexed with God and he left the **Ark of the Covenant** at the house of Obed-Edom the Gittite and went back to the city where he lived.

After three months (perhaps when he was no longer angry), David went and brought the **Ark of the Covenant** to his house personally (the right way). David went ahead of all the men, unlike before he was in the background. David's purpose was to be in front, to be the leader and the one anointed to carry the **Ark of the Covenant**. This is no different from Noah. His purpose was to build an **ARK** that would save him and his family. God chose Noah as the leader and no one else could have done what he did. I can only imagine that many were laughing at Noah when he was building the ark. Noah wasn't building a boat, but an ARK (a cruise ship, in essence). Perhaps God's purpose for you is to build or re-build something and it may seem laughable. One of the things I have learned is that if the vision is easy enough to accomplish then it's not BIG enough.

The Lord anointed David to re-turn the **Ark of the Covenant** to the city of David. It was his Purpose and he needed to walk it out. I've been there, where I was in the background and God was telling me to do something, but instead I would ask my husband to do it or I would share it with others who I believed at the time were more qualified than me. No one else can walk out your purpose except you and no one else is anointed to do what God has told you to do.

It's time to re-calibrate, re-set, re-shuffle some things around, re-route, re-strategize, because your purpose must shine. It's time to take your rightful place in the KINGDOM, because these 7 years at hand, you will need to be in position for the Kingdom Mandate. It's time to be the lender and not the borrower. It's time to own credit unions, be the CFO, the President or Prime Minister, be the Queen or the King, a supreme court judge, own that business, lead the ministry. It's time to live in the **PALACE** Season of your life and reign. Invade your LiFE with the **MEGA**. The time is NOW, says the Lord!

**Moment...................**

What are your Aha moments from this section? What revelation/s did you receive? What will you activate now?

_____

_____

_____

_____

_____

_____

_____

_____

_____

_____

**Prayer:** Pray for God to re-veal to you His PURPOSE for your life, if you don't already know what it is.

**Activation:** Review any prophetic words that you have received. Go back through them because God says He's going to re-veal some things that you missed before. It's time for MEGA MANIFESTATIONS.

_____

_____

_____

_____

_____

_____

_____

_____

_____

_____

_____

_____

# Chapter 7 – Rosh Hashanah

## Head of the Year

On Wednesday, September 20, 2017 at sundown, many Jews and Christians started the celebration of one of the Biblical New Year called **Rosh Hashanah** (Hebrew: ראש השנה), which literally means "head of the year." Jewish days start on sundown/sunset and goes until sundown/sunset the next day. In the book of Genesis, when God completed His work for the day, the scripture says, there was evening and there was morning the first day. *"God called the light "day," and the darkness he called "night." And there was evening, and there was morning---the first day."* Genesis 1:5 NIV. So that's why you will tend to see that Hebraic celebrations starts the evening before the actual day.

Nevertheless, for simplicity purposes, Rosh Hashanah New Year 5778 (Ayin Chet – which I will describe in more details), was fully celebrated on September 21, 2017 on the Gregorian calendar. According to Numbers 29:1 AMP *"On the first day of the seventh month on New Year's Day of the civil year, you shall have a holy summoned assembly; you shall do no servile work. It is a day of blowing of trumpets for you everyone blowing who wishes, proclaiming that the glad New Year has come and that the great Day of Atonement and the Feast of Tabernacles are now approaching."*

Rosh Hashanah is also the first day of the Highest Holy Holiday or Yamim Noraim ("Days of Awe"), which is celebrated for ten days and leads up to what's called **Yom Kippur**, which I will also discuss later on in the text. **Rosh Hashanah** is observed on the first two days of Tishrei, which is the seventh (7th) month of the Hebrew calendar. It is described in the Torah as יום תרועה (Yom Teru'ah, a day of sounding [the Shofar]). You're probably wondering why is a New Year celebrated in the 7th month of the year and not the first month in the year. That's because there are two (2) different Hebraic New Year.

There are two (2) New Year on the Hebraic Calendar. One is called the **Civilian New Year** and the other the **Biblical New Year**. The Civilian New Year is Rosh Hashanah and is believed to be the time when God created Adam and Eve, thus, it's also the celebration of mankind and creation, thanking God for His Creation and for renewing a good year, every year. In fact, one of the sayings that is said at Rosh Hashanah's corporate and personal worship services is that "God would renew for us a good year." The second New Year is Nisan 1 (around March) and Nisan is the first (1$^{st}$) month in the Hebraic Calendar and is considered the Biblical New Year. It's the commemorative of when the children of Israel exiting Egypt – the Great Exodus.

There are also two other minor New Year Tu BiShvat or Tu B'Shevat or Tu B'Shvat (Hebrew: ט״ו בשבט) is a minor Jewish holiday, occurring on the 15th day of the Hebrew month of Shevat (typically January or February on the Gregorian Calendar). It is also called "The New Year of the Trees" or (Hebrew: ראש השנה לאילנות, Rosh HaShanah La'Ilanot). Tu BiShvat is one of four "New Year's" mentioned in the Mishnah. Lastly, a non-celebrated New Year is the 1$^{st}$ day of Elul (August-September) and was celebrated as the tithe of animals when that was a requirement in the early biblical days.

Rosh Hashanah is a time of celebration and feasting and showing gratitude to God for making it to another year. Typically, on Rosh Hashanah, families gather together and feast, have fun and celebrate, just like January 1$^{st}$ in the Gregorian Calendar. Some of the special traditions that take place on Rosh Hashanah are; dipping bread and apples in honey or something sweet.

Our immediate family observes **Rosh Hashanah** as well as the other required feasts. This is one of the most enjoyable time for our children, because they love to bake treats and dip bread and apples in honey. It's just a glorious time and one that all God's people should really partake of because it's required and because speaks volumes to God. Taking time to observe the day, tells God that His timing and seasons are more important to you that your time. It tells Him that you want to have a Good Year and that you need Him to help you have one.

On **Rosh Hashanah**, my immediate family do **NOT** work outside of the home as written in Numbers 29:1, "...*you shall do no servile work...*" If it's a school day, our children do not attend school. While it doesn't say that the children should not attend school, it's really a no-brainer. On January 1st, when the parents don't have work, the children also have no school. Therefore, we follow the same principle.

Since my family and I started observing God's time to the fullest, we have noticed significant blessings in our lives. If you desire to live a life of fullness and joy, then consider meeting up with God for His appointed times. He wants to meet with you. Observing His appointed times come with many blessings and benefits.

There are **Eight** (8) required Feasts and Festivals:

## The Lord's Appointed Times

1. **Sabbath** (Shabbat) – Friday Evening to Saturday Evening
2. **Passover** (Pesach) – 14 Nisan and it's usually around March-April
3. **Unleavened Bread** (Matzo) – 15-21 Nisan (March-April)
4. **FirstFruits to Weeks/Pentecost** (Shavuot) 16 Nisan – 6 Sivan (March-June)
5. **Trumpets** (**Rosh Hashanah**) – 1 Tishrei (September – October)
6. **Day of Atonement** (Yom Kippur) – 10 Tishrei (September – October)
7. **Booths/Tabernacles** (Sukkot) – 15-21 Tishrei (September – October)
8. **Eighth Day of Rejoicing in the Torah** (Simchat Torah) – 22 Tishrei (September – October)

**Added were:**

1. **Lots** (Purim) – based around the story of Esther
2. **Dedication** (Hanukah) – also known as the festival of lights
3. **Ninth of Av** (Tisha B'Av) – remembering when the Temple was destroyed.

There are other times and days of observances, but these are the required appointed times as instructed by God that He wants us to remember them and teach them to our offspring so that the traditions continue. **Rosh Hashanah** is such a wonderful time and If you have never celebrated the Festival and get a chance to blow or hear the blowing of the Shofar, you are missing out. There's an opportunity to partake in the celebration this year on September 10, 2018. Stay connected with me and you can join us live in person or on the internet for Rosh Hashanah 5779.

# NOTES..........

## Times and Seasons

*"Teach us to number our days, that we may gain a heart of wisdom."*
***Psalm 90:12 NIV***

**Understanding Times and Seasons** and biblical numerology may be insignificant to some, but in Judaism and to Prophets they represent God's voice and is one of His languages that He communicates with His people. It is imperative that Christian's understand and know God's timing, because numbers have character and reveal many truths, including understanding the **Torah** (first five books of the Bible), also knows as the Pentateuch. It also reveals that **Jesus Christ** is the Messiah and that He was with God, is God and will return for those that have accepted Him as their personal **Lord and Savior** and have lived a holy life.

Understanding God's timing and seasons and being able to rightly divide the word and see and hear what God is saying requires understanding of both the **Hebraic Calendar** and the **Gregorian Calendar**. They work together and form a horizontal (-) and a vertical (l) line which represents the cross (+). Jesus Christ is never missing from what God is doing, because had it not been for Christ, there would be no revelation from the Holy Spirit and mankind would not have direct access to God.

Transitioning to the Hebraic calendar is not an easy process, so I would suggest starting with observing the **Sabbath Day** and **Rosh Hashanah**. However, you can completely partake of all the Appointed Times that were mentioned in the previous section. God looks at the heart and if He sees your desire to understand His timing then He will guide you along the way. You can also start by purchasing a Messianic

Jewish Calendar that shows both the Hebraic and the Gregorian days and months. This is the calendar that I use. Also, if you have an Apple iPhone, you can add the Hebrew Calendar to your existing calendar app and that's a great start. I don't know if the other smart phones have the Hebrew app as I don't own one.

Look at it this way, when you live according to both calendars, you get to enjoy both worlds, and celebrate three (3) New Years; two (2) on the Hebraic Calendar and one (1) on the Gregorian Calendar. Who doesn't like more reasons to celebrate? Furthermore, when one lives according to God's Calendar, he or she understands what season of life they're in, what season the land is in and what to do during each season. It simply brings more meaning to life and removes any anxiety that you may have.

I don't get raveled up or anxious when I see signs and wonders happening around me, because I know that it's just prophesies being fulfilled. We are living in the end times and having a knowledge of the timing will help you to better prepare and embrace what God is doing. Time is advancing and God is doing some suddenlies. Are you ready to partake with what He's doing?

There are so many mysteries and revelations that are found in the written word of God that has to do with timing, numbers and seasons. For example, the first place in the Bible that the word heal or any variation of healing/health appears is **Genesis 20:17**. Nowhere in the written word of God before Genesis 20, verse 17 will you find the word heal. In the year 2017, I wrote a book called Heal-thy LiFE™, Heal-thy Land that became a best seller (internationally) within one hour of launching it.

God revealed to me and I wrote an entire book about this, that the year 2017 was a year of healing, many victories and that the year 2017 restarted the healing process. While on Tour, we witnessed many healing miracles, such as marriages restored, tumors shrinked, cancer healed, the deaf was able to hear and so much more. New in 2018, is the 2$^{nd}$ edition of the book with updated stories and it can be found here:
Https://www.amazon.com/author/carolynganderson

The point is, there are mysteries and hidden revelations in the word of God that will help you understand times and seasons. Before the foundations of the world, God knew that He would reveal the **Year 2017** as the **MVP Year** and the Year of many healing, considering that Genesis 20:17 existed before the beginning of time. God also knew that there would be a Prophet in place that He could reveal His mystery to. God has many revelations that He wants to reveal to you, so it's time to get in position and focus on hearing what God is saying.

 **Moment……….**

One of the missing blessings in most of the Christian community is to truly operate according to God's calendar. Christians will become unstoppable, more powerful and a force to be reckon with if they would tap into God's timing and seasons and enjoy the blessings of being truly engrafted into the royal family.

Unfortunately, so many Christians do not know that they have a unique gift by having the ability to live according to the Hebraic and the Gregorian calendar. This gives more days to celebrate life and honor God. Looks like it's time for a SHIFT!

## Numbers & Biblical Numerology

Have you ever read a passage of scripture and noticed that the scripture is repeated? That is not by accident or coincidence, as there's no such thing with God. When God repeats himself, He's making a point. He's really attempting to get our attention to realize that the matter is very important. There are also times when certain numbers show up frequently, and that is also not coincidental. The bible is the blueprint for life and every answer that one needs can be found there.

Biblical Numerology and numbers are very important, but they are not magic or to be mis-interpreted. Biblical Numerology requires interpretation and sound analyzing and understanding from the Holy Spirit. For example, many have read Genesis 20:17, over and over again, including myself, but it wasn't until God was ready to reveal about healing and Gen: 20:17

that it became significant. The scripture existed before you and me, but it had to be the right timing for the revelation. Sometimes understanding the revelation takes time, prayer and fasting. At other times, it helps to ask other Prophets what they are sensing, especially those who God has given the grace and the gift to understand biblical numerology.

*"My people are destroyed from lack of knowledge."*
**Hosea 4:6 NIV**

The bible says that we are destroyed from a lack of knowledge and this indeed is true. The lack of knowledge and understanding of God's times and seasons can destroy one's destiny. I was being destroyed when I didn't have the knowledge of God's timing and seasons and now that I know, I do differently. I was alive, but I wasn't living.

Everything that God does, the enemy always attempt to create a look alike but it's always a counterfeit. The enemy has tainted the blessing that comes with true numerology and understanding mysteries and hidden codes in the written word of God. The enemy has twisted it into witchcraft and fortunetelling. He has his own false prophetic team, psychic's and tarot readers, who claim to be able to share future occurrences by reading palms and performing other satanic acts. They even attempt to make economic predictions, but always fail, because truth always trump lies. The enemy's counterfeit will never succeed, because God only reveals His Plans to His servants, the Prophets (Amos 3:7), and not to those who do NOT belong to Him.

I hope the contents in this book bring revelations and enlightenment of the importance of living according to God's timing. God's covenant and His promises belong to those that have chosen Jesus Christ (Yeshua) as Lord and Savior. This is the year to not let the promises pass you by. It's the **MEGA Year** and God is **Making Everything Good Again**. Are you ready? Numbers are so significant to God that there's an entire book in the bible titled **Numbers**.

**Pause Moment......................**

Pause and take a moment and review Chapter 7. Write down what you've learned about **Rosh Hashanah and the Appointed Times**. Reflect on what you've learned about **Times and Seasons**. This moment is all about you. Write down any **Aha moment** or revelation that you received.

_____

_____

_____

_____

_____

_____

_____

_____

# Chapter 8 – The Year 5778

## Ayin Chet

Welcome to **Ayin Chet**, the Hebraic Year **5778** – the year to see with the mind and not with the physical eyes. It's the year of the Open Door and the year of New Beginnings. As stated before, numbers are very significant to God, whether in the Hebraic or the Gregorian Calendar. On the Hebraic Calendar however, not only do the Years have significant meanings, they have names with numerical values.

**Ayin** is the 16th letter of the Hebrew alphabet (Aleph-Bet) and represents the numeric value of seventy. Therefore, since the turn of the 70's in the Hebraic Calendar, each year starts off as Ayin plus, (whatever the other numerical value is). For example, last year 5777 (2017) was Ayin-Zayin (the number 7), thus, creating seventy-seven (77), using only the two last numbers of the year. This year 5778 is Ayin Chet (the number eight) creating 57-78.

It is similar to describing what the number 18 means for the year 2018. Very rarely the 20 is talked about, but rather the last two numbers. Both the Hebraic and the Gregorian Calendars are coming to an end in its strain that it is in. Pretty soon, it will be 57-80 and 20-20, and the re-start of counting of the years 1-9, such as 81 and 21. It is going to be a rather interesting and exciting cycle.

# Here's an image of the basic Hebrew Alphabet

Image credit: www.hebrew4christians.com

Hebraic Alphabet numbers are easy to understand because it always comes with a pictorial meaning. The pictorial meaning of Ayin (other than 70) is eye and it is used to note vision or insight. Ayin is a letter that also denotes critical points in history and perfect spiritual order.

The word Ayin also represent the primeval light, that is the spiritual light of God mentioned in Genesis 1:3, which is different from the celestial light of God mentioned in Genesis 1:14-18. According to the Jewish midrash, God's spiritual light is far greater than the light from the sun and the stars (www.hebrew4christians.com). This means that during the years of Ayin, any darkness that is hidden in your life, can be broken by decreeing "let there be light" and standing on the word of God. Let the Ayin years of your life be brightened and let your light shine.

**NOTES..........**

_____

_____

_____

_____

_____

_____

_____

# The Year of the Open Door

 *Chet*

The eighth letter of the Hebrew Alphabet is Chet (sounds like mate). The pictorial image for Chet resembles a door, a wall or a fence. The year 5778 gives access to THE OPEN DOOR, one door, not to be confused with open doors. There are times when God allows doors to be opened in our lives, but this is NOT the kind of open door that is taking place this year. It is just one door. According to John 10:9 AMPC it reads *"I am the Door; anyone who enters in through Me will be saved (will live). He will come in and he will go out freely, and will find pasture."* The Door has been opened and Jesus Christ is the way. This is a year when only those who have entered the door will have the opportunity to experience the #**MEGA LiFE**.

**Pause Moment......................**

Pause and take a moment and review Chapter 8. Write down what you have learned about Ayin Chet and the year 5778. In summary, Ayin Chet is the year to see with the mind and to walk through the **Door of LiFE**. It is time for you to access all the blessings that's in store for you.

_____

_____

_____

_____

_____

_____

_____

# Chapter 9 –Happy New Year

Every January 1<sup>st</sup> of the Gregorian calendar it's New Year's Day, which is the only New Year that's a part of the Gregorian Calendar, unlike the Hebraic Calendar that has two (2) New Year. It's normally a fun and exciting time and most people seem to be mostly in good spirits. Some will share their goals and aspirations for the new year on social media and other communication outlets. Instead of goals, others will say that they are making new year's resolutions and they seem very confident and proud that this new year will be the year that all things great shall happen.

There are some typical traditions that usually take place during the new year, such as: some people attend a New Year's Eve church service, while others host parties or travel to New York City to see the New Year's Eve ball drop. Some simply stay at home and watch television and bring in the new year with their family.

Lots of weddings and marriage proposals also take place on New Year's Eve/Day and sometimes some break-ups. While there are several festivities and traditions that takes place on January 1$^{st}$, there are no specific written instructions or guidelines written in the word of God for the celebration of January 1$^{st}$ as there is for Rosh Hashanah or any of the Hebraic New Year.

Therefore, since I am very aware of how important days and times are to God, my immediate family and I and those that I am connected to, have instituted our own traditions for January 1st. First, we stay home for the night of celebration, or if we are away (very rarely), we still stay together in a home setting. It's our belief that you should welcome the new year with family and be at home if possible.

We host our Church's New Year's Eve Celebration from 8pm to 10pm so that the members and followers will have time to embrace the new year with their families. This is the same tradition that's practiced in Judaism. There's a worship gathering at the temple or at a community center and there's singing and dancing and the families go home to continue the celebration.

At midnight on New Year's Eve, our family make decrees and declarations that we are expecting to have, such as declaring that it shall be a good year. By December 31st, I would have shared with my family what the New Year is all about, because God usually shares with me the meaning of the year since Rosh Hashanah (around September - October) of the preceding year. Our children love the celebrations, because a big part of it includes making treats, having fun, and cooking some of their favorite dishes.

On January $1^{st}$, there's a specific process that we follow for goal setting and usually by the end of January we have completed our **Manifestation Maps**™ and are ready to activate the word of the Lord for the year. Personally, for me, one of my goals for the month of January is to finish the book for the year, as I did for this book. Typically, I launch the book for the year on January $31^{st}$ of the given year. This is also when I start the Tour for the Word of the Lord.

This year **2018** is an extremely historic moment in time, because it's the year when God is **Making Everything Good Again (MEGA)**.

It's the year of separating **Light** from **Darkness**, the Year of **LiFE** and the year of New Beginnings. It is also the year of starting the seven (7) year cycle of **Abundance** as it was in the days of Joseph the Dreamer. I hope you are as excited as I am, because it is indeed a **GRAND, MEGA YEAR**.

NOTES..........

_____

_____

_____

_____

_____

_____

_____

_____

# Chapter 10 –MEGA Year 2018

Making Everything Good Again

**NOW**! The moment that you have been waiting for. It's time for the great reveal of what this **#MEGA YEAR** is all about. I have been anticipating writing this chapter because it is so **MEGA.** This is the year when God is <u>Making Everything Good Again</u>. This is absolutely one of the best years ever and yes, you have probably heard that before, but hopefully from reading the previous chapters, you have noticed that seasons, times and days, all belong to God and that it's very important to him. As Bishop T.D. Jakes would say "get ready, get ready, get ready."

The year **2018** is the **MEGA** year and if you haven't figured it out yet, the acronym **MEGA** stands for **Making Everything Good Again and** also **Making Every-day Good Again**. This is the year when God is taking us back to **Genesis** and making all things new in Earth. Everything God made, He saw that it was good and if everything He made was good then every day that He also made is a good day.

Everyday should be a day of expecting Good-News, because since Christ was with God since the beginning, it means that everything, every day, every life, every moment in God, are all good things and good days. According to Genesis 1:18 NIV, it says that *"...And God saw that it was good."* First God spoke *"let there be"* and then He saw that what He created was good. You are God's good creation and you're living in a good time. Just like God, one has to speak (declare) what you want to see in your life.

Last year in 5777/2017 – the **MVP Year**, God completed most of His resetting, because things and people's lives had gotten out of control. This was not God's first reset and it probably won't be His last before the return of Christ. However, 2017 was a year of the Re's. Reset's are significant because it allows things to start new and fresh again. In the book of Acts, verses 3:19, 21, NIV, it describes how God is always restoring and refreshing. He does this, because again, it is NOT God's will that people should perish.

> *"Repent, then, and turn to God, so that your sins may be wiped out, that times of refreshing may come from the Lord, Heaven must receive him until the time comes for God to **restore everything**, as he promised long ago through his holy prophets."*

Reset's are not new set of phenomenon's as they are clearly written in the Word of God. Reset's can be personal, geographical, cultural or even global. A very specific global and obvious reset took place during the days of Noah, when God created a **new beginning** after the flood. This is one of the reasons why the number eight (8) is said to be the number of new beginnings. God started mankind all over again with eight people, namely; Noah and his wife, their three (3) sons and their wives. They were the chosen family during that timeframe that God made all things new again. He washed away all the corruption and sin, because He can only tolerate foolishness for so long. God is the same God then, today and forevermore and once again, God is instituting a new beginning.

Another major reset was the death and resurrection of Jesus Christ. God sent His Son to die for you and me, that through Him, we would be restored, redeemed and be engrafted back into God's family. Mankind was heading in the wrong direction, and Christ became the pause moment, the RESET, that would give us life again. Due to

His redemptive power, there's a new start, a new beginning, an upgraded life. God used 2017 as a year that He performed some resets in people's lives and prophetically, there were three (3) major resets that I wrote about in the book (2017 The MVP Year). It was imperative that these resets took place to get things and lives back in order. These resets needed to happen to prepare for the Year of New Beginnings, the Year of Light, the Year of Life, The Year of the Open Door and the Year of the **MEGA**.

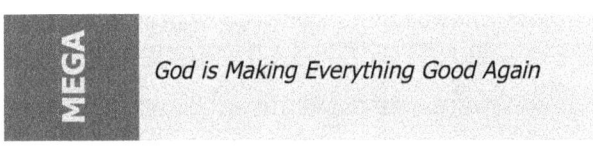

God is Making Everything Good Again

There are also natural resets, such as new leadership positions, new presidents, new seasons and so forth that all took place and probably will continue to take place. I wrote about the Remnants and a changing of the guards earlier in the text. God is handing the baton to the people and the generation that should be in leadership positions today. Not all leaders effectively passed the baton. Some of them held on to it, even to their graves. Again, God's will must always be done, and if He has to move people out the way so that His creation, plan and order continues, so that the law of Multiplication continues, then that's what He will do.

Recently, I purchased a new iPhone and it started experiencing some problems. The technician instructed me to reset the phone so that it can be restored to its original state with new software. After I followed this process, the phone started working much better and the problems were resolved. This is what a reset is all about. It allows things to become new all over again, with upgrades and improvement so that things can work the way they should. God is doing some major upgrades and those who are alive will get to see the manifestations of it! It's the **MEGA**

Year, actually it's also the **MEGA** Cycle (seven (7) years of Abundance. It shall be glorious and it's time to get in position and maximize your gifts, talents and abilities for what God has in store for you.

Now that the major resets are over, God is re-establishing His order and making everything good again. I used to thing that **Great** was a better word than Good, until I heard a Pastor say that the ultimate position of God is Him being a **Good God**. This helped me to understand why in the book of Genesis, after God made everything, He **saw** that it was good and not that it was great. It's not that greatness is not an awesome state, because it is, but there's a reason why God said it was good and not that it was great. God's best is when He say it is Good. Making Everything Good Again is both a spiritual and a natural new beginning. Just think, every day, every month, every quarter, every season, every year, is an opportunity for you to experience and walk in God's newness. I speak newness into every area of your life.

There are six (6) times in the first Chapter of Genesis that **God** saw that what He made was **good** and one (1) time **very good** to total seven (7) times, which represents completion and His divine perfection. The following verses describes God's vision of Him seeing everything he made as being good:

> **Genesis 1:1,4,10,12,18,21,25,31 NIV**
>
> "In the beginning God created the heavens and the earth. [4] God saw that the light was **good**, and he separated the light from the darkness. [10] God called the dry ground "land," and the gathered waters he called "seas." And God saw that it was **good**. [12] The land produced vegetation: plants bearing seed according to their kinds and trees bearing fruit with seed in it according to their kinds. And God saw that it was **good**. [18] to govern the day and the night, and to separate light from darkness. And God saw that it was **good**. [21] So God created the great creatures of the sea and every

living thing with which the water teems and that moves about in it, according to their kinds, and every winged bird according to its kind. And God saw that it was **good**. [25] God made the wild animals according to their kinds, the livestock according to their kinds, and all the creatures that move along the ground according to their kinds. And God saw that it was **good**. [31] God saw all that he had made, and it was **very good**. And there was evening, and there was morning---the sixth day."

## In the beginning, God made the following:

Day 1: Let there be Light!

Day 2: Sky (Separated the waters above from below)

Day 3: Fruits, Vegetables and Trees

Day 4: Sun, Moon, Stars

Day 5: Fish and Birds

Day 6: Animals and Mankind

Day 7: He rested (Sabbath Day)

As God began to reveal to me the complete meaning of the #**MEGA** Year, He kept saying "all things new in 2018." This is the year to speak newness and light into your life. Anytime something old or past things attempt to re-surface in your life, declare that "all things are new." Declare "let there be light." Anything that is dark or not clear, should not be in your life. If you see darkness showing up in your life, don't accept it, instead reject it.

Personally, I was planning to get another used (new to me) vehicle to replace the one that I have now, and God said, nope "all things new in 2018." Do not get a used vehicle, but get one that is brand new. He didn't' have to tell me twice, I said "okay Lord." This means that God will be providing financial provision so that I can buy the new vehicle with cash, because I don't plan on financing anything in the **MEGA** Year or ever, unless it's a strategic reason, like business credit.

One of the new things that God showed me, was that there shall be many marriages, and re-marriages, new homes, new purchases, new friends, new career, new levels of anointing's, new gifts, new territories and new relationships and so forth. There shall be many things new in 2018 and beyond. Actually, the year 2018 and 2019 go hand in hand and are connected to the year 2020. I will speak about this during my Tour.

*"In the beginning was the Word, and the Word was with God, and the Word was God. He was with God from the beginning."*
**John 1:1-2 NIV**

God is making all things new and pure as it was in the beginning. There was an increase of darkness like it was in the beginning and during all the reset period. Now God is saying, let there be light. Whenever light shows up in your life, it can only be good. Light exposes darkness and light brings life. Jesus Christ is the light of the world and when He's in your life, there can be no darkness.

God took His time and created all that is needed for mankind to survive. He gave fruits, vegetables, trees, fishes, animals, plants and light. He provided instructions about what to eat and what not to eat. All things were good in the beginning. Life was pure and communication with God was good. The bible says that God communed with Adam in the cool of the day. It would have continued down that path, had sin not became a part of Adam and Eve's life.

The choice they made changed the trajectory of their offspring. Christ had to be sent to redeem mankind because He was with God and is God and knows first-hand about God's divine plan. Now God is redeeming us again, and this time, He's starting all over and making everything good again. God loves us so much that He has chosen **5778/2018** to be the beginning of making things new again. Part of the process of making things new requires a separation of light and darkness. There will be a difference between those who are of the light and those who represent darkness. There is no getting around this in the #**MEGA** Year and the #**MEGA** Cycle.

## Light vs. Darkness

*"God saw that the light was good, and he separated the light from the darkness."*

**Genesis 1:4 NIV**

Everything in life is a process. From the foundations of the world God created the heaven's and the earth by applying a process. According to Genesis 1:1-3, it says:

> **"In the beginning God created the heavens and the earth. Now the earth was formless and empty, darkness was over the surface of the deep, and the Spirit of God was hovering over the waters. And God said, "Let there be light," and there was light."**

God will be separating light from darkness. Those who are on the fence or in the middle (lukewarm), will need to choose to be hot or cold, light or darkness. There are some who call themselves Christians, but are living according to the world's standard of life. Christianity is more than attending church or being a part of the choir. It is an everyday lifestyle and the light should shine in everything that a Christian does.

God has been very patient and He has given many, an opportunity to get it right. He has extended extra Grace (it seems) during 2015 and 2016 - the Spin Cycle Years and in 2017 - the

Reset Year. He doesn't want to see His creation perish. He wants to see everyone saved. Unfortunately, the decision of whether or not one perishes or don't is contingent on choices that each person make. Consequently, it's not too late. There's always an opportunity for repentance and forgiveness, always. However, there comes a point when God has to separate light from darkness. It is inevitable. There came a point when He had to destroy Sodom and Gomorrah and started a new lifestyle for Lot and his family. Once again God is now looking for those who are ready to live life fully every day, forever.

## Number 8 (Infinity)

The number eight (8) is also the symbol of **Infinity** and represents infinite blessings, abundance, overflow and **MEGA**. The number represents everything that is ultimately good and because it has no ending point, it demonstrates that it's a continuous blessing. It is a divine number that also represents vision. This type of vision is being able to see with the mind and not with the eyes. It is a profound number because it's the number that God uses for new beginnings. After He created the heavens and the earth in six (6) days, and rested on the Sabbath (Seventh) day, the eighth ($8^{th}$) day was the day of new beginnings. This is the season to focus on God's infinite promises, God cannot lie and He stands by His words, so if He said it, it is so! It's the beginning of a new life for His chosen ones.

## Year of Chai (Life)

In Hebrew, Chai is the number 18 and it means life or living. It is customary in Jewish culture that they give money in multiples of 18 as a means of giving life. If there's ever a time to live life to the fullest, using all the gifts and talents that you have been given, it's now.

Are you ready for a change? Are you ready to live the ultimate **#MEGA LiFE™**? Are you ready to be the best you, to let your light shine, to start all over again, to experience God's very best, to step into your cycle of Abundance? Are you ready to **Live it Fully Everyday**, the definition of (**LiFE**)? If you answered (yes) to any of the questions above, let me say <u>congratulations</u>! You are ready for the infinite blessings that are awaiting you. If you said yes, then you are fired up and ready to live life to the fullest potential, having no limitations.

In order to live the **#MEGALiFE**, one has to first make a decision that they are ready for the change. Since all things are becoming new, one cannot do the same things as the past. He or she cannot live or have a mindset of the past or not even the future, but it must be in the present moment. One must maximize his or her every day, because really, that's all we have. Every day is a new day to start a new life.

Every day is a gift from God and should not be taken for granted, because it is not promised. Therefore, the minute you realize that you have the breath of life and that you are alive, consider it a good day. You are alive in the timeframe of infinite blessings and new beginnings. Both the Hebraic and the Gregorian calendar ends with the number eight, therefore embrace your new beginnings.

Chet which is the Hebrew number for eight (8) which I wrote about also means life. Therefore, God is saying very loud and clear that this is the year of life and the year to truly start living. It's the year to let your light also shine, because that is what life is truly about. It's the year when one should truly walk in his or her purpose. This is the year to truly know what you are called or chosen to be and to do. I believe for many it's the Palace Time. This is the time when things stabilize in your life. The Palace Time is when you step into your purpose, you have more than enough and not struggling or merely surviving. It's time to leave the Prison season of your life, because you've been there long enough. Activate your new life, change your clothes and prepare to enter the Palace Season/Time of your life.

## NOTES..........

Please jot down your thoughts and takeaways from **Chapter 10**. This was a powerful chapter that dug deep into what the MEGALiFE, the number 18 and number 8 are all about. This is your Pause, Reflect and Write Moment. It belongs to you. You may be eager to move on; however, reflection brings revelations.

_____

_____

_____

_____

_____

_____

_____

# Chapter 11 - Palace Time

Image Credit: Joshua Ivan Sudrajat

Life is a Journey filled with seasons, cycles and very few live in a state of TIME. Seasons exist within cycles and cycles exist within TIME. Seasons are cycles or cyclical but TIME is Constant and Dimensional. For example, when Joseph went to live in the Palace it was his time to rule and reign. Yet his time would be broken down into 7-year cycles, which were the **Seven years of Abundance** and 7 years of famine. Within those seven years, each year had 4 different seasons and each season, had months, weeks, days, hours and seconds. However, no matter what season or cycle Joseph was going through, once he entered the **PALACE** he stepped into the season of Time. This was when his true purpose manifest. Joseph remained in the palace for the rest of his life. This is when life shifts to a new level and one starts living in TIME. Decree that when you have entered or is entering your Palace Season and that you will NOT go back to the old ways of living.

This is the **#MEGA YEAR** when God is **Making Everything Good Again**. He doesn't desire for you to be complacent, stagnant, depressed, broken or broke. Instead, His desire is that you would prosper and be in good health. He desires that you will be filled with joy, happiness, peace and contentment.

It's a time for Elevation, **MEGA** and Wealth. It's time for you to use the gifts and talents that God gave you to take your rightful place in the Kingdom of God. It's time for you to use your delegated authority and be on the command post. In one of my books from the **Pit to the Palace**, I share that all life's experiences that we go through is to get us tough enough and equipped to lead like Joseph and to see the manifestations of God's promises. God always have an appointed time for everything and no man or devil can stop it. God's set and appointed time to live the **MEGA** life and enter the **PALACE season and TIME** is at hand.

It is in the **PALACE** that Joseph would live for the rest of his life and this is where the 7-year cycle within TIME began. Joseph had 7 good years and the 7 not so good years, but he was never without and the people came to him for their food supply. So, shall it be for YOU and ME. The transfer of wealth is here, but you must be prepared. From the beginning, God knew that this season would come. He knew that you would be alive at this present moment to see His divine timetable playing out.

## Wealth Transfer

*"And I will make the Egyptians favourably disposed toward this people, so that when you leave you will not go empty handed."*
***Exodus 3:21 NIV***

Since the time of Exodus from EGYPT, there has not been a major transfer of Wealth for God's People. This also means that since the time when Christ was on earth and ascended there hasn't been a major WEALTH TRANSFER either. I believe that the time is NOW. According to Exodus 3:20-22 NIV it states ***"So I will stretch out my hand and strike the Egyptians with all the wonders that I will perform among them. After that, he will let you go. "And I will make the Egyptians favorably disposed toward*** *this people, so that when you leave you will not go empty-handed. Every woman is to ask her neighbor and any woman living in her house for articles of silver and gold and for clothing, which you will put on your sons and daughters. And so, you will plunder the Egyptians."*

This major Wealth Transfer requires a process just like it was in the days of the Exodus. God has already started the process that's needed for the WEALTH transfer. First, He did some cleansing in 2016, many victories and healing in 2017 and now it's time for the New Beginnings and to step into a Wealthy Place. It's time for the unhealthy life to EXODUS. It's time for it to go! You can have complete wealth in your mind and body, finance, faith and relationships. Wealth is more than finances, considering that "True Wealth starts with your Health in mind." The Wealth Transfer is overdue.

WEALTH was transferred to Joseph because he went through the **process** that led to him walking out his PURPOSE. Purpose is a journey and not a destination. Joseph went from being chosen, the most favored son to being in slavery, accusation and prison. From there he was promoted to the Palace. Your prayers are about to be answered. God is saying that as you prepare yourself in the prison season, where your GIFT makes room for you and in no time, you shall reap what you have sown.

In Acts 12:12-16 NIV, while the people were praying for Peter to be released from Prison, an Angel of the Lord released Peter and he went and knocked at the door to announce his release. God is releasing you from your pain, suffering, prison season and from debt because you've knocked at the door and it's time for it to be OPENED.

The major transfer will take place when you STEP into your PURPOSE. What were you created to be? Just like anything in life there's a process to get to the result. Moses had to go through a process to redeem the children of Israel. David had to walk through a process to rule in the palace. I had to go through a process to get to where I am today and so shall you.

Get ready! You are about to experience a major Wealth Transfer if you have been in position and prepared for it. Get ready for the overnight promotions from the Prison season to the Palace season. Walk in your year of the **MEGALiFE**™, in your year of light, and the Year of the Open Door. It's time to Awaken your life and live the best life you've ever lived. Now is not the time to fall asleep or to let others pass you by. Now is not the time for you to be burdened down with problems, depression, confusion or despair. It's the time to rejoice. It's the time to shout. It's the time to take down all the giants in your life and be awakened.

# NOTES..........

Take a moment and reflect on Chapter 11 and journal the journey. What season of life do you believe you are in?

# Chapter 12 – The Awakening

*"Awake, harp and lyre! I will awaken the dawn."*
***Psalm 108:2 NIV***

For the last few years, I have been hearing stories of revivals and awakenings and a great big change that's coming. My husband and I are very familiar with awakenings as we've been ministering about the awakening for the last six (6) years. The great BIG change that Prophets have been declaring that's coming, is actually here NOW. Since one of the gifts of the Prophet is to foretell and to see ahead of time, what can happen is, they continue to declare what's coming and don't see that what they were saying is coming, is actually here. Their prophecies were fulfilled and now it's time to lead the people in the manifestation of the prophecies. It's time to strategize and work the prophecies, per se.

God released an awakening strategy that you can participate in. He has already qualified and equipped you to pursue your rightful position in the Kingdom. According to Colossians 1:2 AMP ***"Giving thanks to the Father, Who has qualified and made us fit to share the portion which is the inheritance of the saints (God's holy people) in the Light."*** Therefore, the time is now for you to activate your influence and maximize what you have been gifted to carry out. Earth needs you to occupy your space and pursue your purpose and take dominion.

## THE AWAKENING STRATEGY

- ✓ **Apostles** – The anointing of an Apostle is to plant, build and re-build churches, ministries, cities, nations and families. Apostles are responsible for being overseer's and leading leaders.

- ✓ **Prophets** - laying the foundation and being the leading voice that God uses to establish His Plans. It's more than bringing a prophetic word to the people. It's about being a leader and working together to re-build God's foundation. They are to travel and prophesy what thus says the Lord and not necessarily be in the four (4) walls of the local church.

- ✓ **Evangelist** - spreading the word of God on the highways and byways, going into homes and ministering the word of God. Stirring up the spirit of God in the people. True Evangelism is about going into the world. It's not necessarily about preaching in the church, but rather sharing the Good-News to those who are lost.

- ✓ **Pastors** - ministering to the people, being a shepherd over the sheep. Pastor of different groups to those assigned to them. Oftentimes the leader of a congregation is referred to as the Pastor and while that may last for a service time, it becomes overwhelming if that congregation has over 50 people. It will become chaotic and out of order. When there were multitudes that needed to be fed, Jesus instructed His disciples to have the people sit down in groups of fifty, Luke 9:14. The Pastor cannot shepherd the people, acts as the administrator and is expected to bring a weekly sermon that will impact and inspire the lives of the congregants. This is not possible and that is why so many congregations seem (dead) and stagnant, because the people aren't growing. Therefore, it's time to separate the congregation with multiple Pastors who lead different groups and having overseers such as Apostles and Prophets that help to build up the church and teachers that teach.

- ✓ **Teachers** - rightly dividing the word. Teaching the Word of God for understanding and revelation.

- ✓ **Revivals** – hosting revivals for the saints (can't revive something that was never birth) focus on reviving the Christians or the backsliders.

- ✓ **Missionaries** - going on a mission to help the sick, poor and the homeless and visiting those in hospitals. Helping the orphans, widows and those less fortunate. Missionaries are not to be in the four walls preaching. This is where they come to be re-fueled. A Missionary is a full-time work and so you should have systems set up in place that provides financial support as you go on the journey.

- ✓ **Intercessors and Prayer Warriors-** praying strategic prayers until they see breakthrough. Intercessors are so powerful and can be sometimes an overlooked group. They carry the heart of God and have a special place in His heart. They are one of the most needed ministries in Christendom today.

- ✓ **Gifts** - Each Christian using their gifts and talents in the KINGDOM (whether marketplace or in the physical church).

- ✓ **Adopt a Block** -**Transform a City** going into the neighborhoods to clean (one block at a time) build trust, show and tell (show God by loving the un-loving and helping the less fortunate and then tell Christ). Provide basic human needs first and then share the good news.

- ✓ **Chaplains** - Police Chaplains, Disaster Chaplains, Sex & Human Trafficking etc. Marketplace Chaplains working full time in Corporate firms.

- ✓ **Safe Havens/Group Homes** - homes for the poor, widow, abused, lost, homeless, broken. Christian's purchasing the homes and turning them into shelters or group homes.

- ✓ **Workplace Chaplains** - getting into the workplace and becoming a part of the leadership team. Go on the inside as an undercover so that he or she can become an influencer and make moral and godly decisions that affects the people.

## The Ten (10) Spheres of Influence
## Similar to the 7 Mountains + 3

1. **Businesses** - supporting Christian led businesses. Starting your own business. Becoming the next CEO, Leader, Executive etc. **Only** use your money to purchase and support companies that you believe in and has the same values as you do.

2. **Arts/Entertainment** - Christian Entertainment, Songs and Music for the NOW GENERATION that edifies GOD. Talk Shows and Public Figures that represents Christ. Going into the Arts and having your talents and skills to demonstrate creativity.

3. **Family** – restoring Kingdom Families, Getting the fathers back into the homes, Marriages between one man and one woman, protecting the entity of family, and standing for justice.

4. **Government** - praying for the leaders. Become a government official or politician yourself so that you can be the decision maker and perhaps the next president of the nation where you reside. Laws that protect families and matters important to Christians. Getting into the systems and becoming the next government officials.

5. **Education** – building our own Kingdom Schools, where the children are taught biblical history and learn who they are at an early age. We need prayer back into the schools and for someone to take the mantle and fight to get back prayers in schools. We need real Kingdom Universities and Colleges, that are teaching economic principles from a biblical perspective.

6. **Religion/Ministry** – it's time to break down the boundaries and barriers of religion that have left many people bound. Man-made rules and regulations have taken the place of sound biblical teaching and have pushed many away from the church. It's time to bring the prodigals back and teach and show them true love, because God is love. Churches will not look the way that it always has, as there's a new way to have church that's being birth right now.

7. **Media** – Time to share the GOOD NEWS! It is time for us to not implode our homes with all the negativity that's happening in and around the world, but to have more Christian news stations, sharing and spreading the good that's happening in the world. We can do this! It's time for Kingdom Citizens to go into the world of Media and be an Ambassador for God.

8. **Science & Technology** – the technological world is different from media. Media is an outlet (whether social media of broadcast television), but technology exist in every area

of life. Whether it is drones, or the latest smart phone, or the ability to go paperless and be all digital, technology is its own spheres of influence. Are you called to that area? Are you called to dominate a space in the technological field? Look at Facebook and Amazon and other products and companies, they are making millions, from a simple vision, an idea, a concept and today they are living the dream. You can do the same.

9. **Healthcare** – this sphere of influence is what I refer to as the undercover secret agent. From working in healthcare on the insurance side, I know first-hand some of what goes on behind closed doors. There's also healthcare on the clinical side, such as hospitals and clinics. The healthcare mountain per se is one of the most influential spheres of influence. One cannot survive without their health, right? Most medications were not intended to get you well, because how else would the pharmaceutical companies make money? They were intended to keep you coming back (maintenance drugs are what they are called). There are some that are necessary, but shouldn't be a lifetime dependency. Nevertheless, there are good things that happen and can happen within this sphere, such as scientists researching for the

latest breakthrough cure. Wellness Coaches helping people become better. Are you called to be a doctor, a wellness coach, a fitness instructor and the like? There's healing for every disease. By His Stripes we are healed. Therefore, you can minister healing to see families become whole.

10. **Finance** – While Finance exist within all the Spheres of Influence, the 10 Mountains, considering that money is needed for everything, it's still necessary to be its own mountain because there are people that are gifted with the ability to understand finance and commerce. Are you called to open up a Credit Union and have the money being managed in your system? What about the banking industry, do you see yourself being the head of some of the financial institutions? What about being a prophetic financial advisor, where you can predict the stock market and guide God's people about creating profitable portfolios? There's so many opportunities in any of the area.

These are just some examples of ways that you can occupy your space and walk out your purpose in life. More than likely your purpose falls within one of those spheres of influence above. Therefore, it's time for you to **OCCUPY** your space and use your gift to make room for you and others. You were born to lead.

NOTES..........

**Time to Pause…and use the space below to write down what you have learned from this Chapter. What will you apply immediately? What were some aha moments for you? What did you learn that you didn't know before? Which of the Ten (10) spheres of influence do you believe you are called to? Note, it could be more than one.**

# Summary

 *"...And God saw that it was good."*
**Genesis 1:18 NIV**

Whew! What a good book! Wow! This is such an impactful book that I will personally read it over again and again. God's voice is permeating earth through the insights and revelations that He gave in this text. I suggest that you go back through and read this again. Similar to the Bible, when you read it again, there's different revelations that are received after the $2^{nd}$ or $3^{rd}$ time after reading the text. It was a difficult book for me to write, not because writing is difficult, but because of some of the deep insights and revelations that I was getting and I had to decide what to include now, and what to include in later books.

Nevertheless, you have more than enough content in this text to last you more than a year. I know that this book will be another best-seller, because of its practically and accuracy. People are looking for a change, a fresh start, a new beginning and they're wanting to hear what God has to say. God is speaking very loud and clear. The only way to hear God is to clear the clutter from your mind and focus on what He's telling you to do. If any of the content in this text was a confirmation to something that God or another Prophet told you, then you no longer need to be praying about it, but rather to activate it, because it serves as a witness to you.

The book started off by introducing you to the **MEGA** Year and giving you Background Information about Dr. Carolyn and about the previous years and why God is doing what He's doing now. The purpose of the book was shared so that you have a clear understanding of what this book is all about. It's one thing to be introduced to a text, but without purpose, one does not know where he or she is going.

The Preface included a look-back at the Spin Cycle and the Reset Years. It was necessary to share this as a precursor to what God is doing today, after all, today is all we have. Chapter One goes into specific details about the Spin Cycle Year **2016** and how God had to squeeze some heaviness out of His people in preparation for the **MVP Year of 2017**. This was the year of Manifestations, Victo-ries (the Re's) and Purposes and Promises being established. God performed many Reset's during the Year 2017.

This book then introduced you to the Hebraic Calendar and provided a broad overview of the year 5776 and 5777. It shared the differences between the Hebraic Calendar and the

Gregorian Calendar and how God uses both calendars to execute and establish His Plans. In essence, God's people are in this world but not of this world, meaning that, while we understand that the world has its own system and standards we are keenly aware of who's standard to live by.

There's a new leadership arising and also has risen. They are the ones that God has given authority to lead in this time. We are called the **REMNANTS** as mentioned in Genesis 45:7.

Chapter Five (5) was what I called one of the **defining moments chapter** as it helps to bring clarity about one's purpose. Here it was shared that this is a season when one will need to truly know his or her purpose in life and live that life fully every day. This is a huge part of living in the **2018 MEGA** Year. The late Dr. Myles Munroe said**, "The greatest tragedy in life is not death, but life without meaning, without a purpose."**

Therefore, it's time to truly live life with meaning. It's important to know where you fit in, within the Ten spheres of influence, also referred to as the seven mountains and actually I have added three (3) more areas to the existing seven. It is a great time to be alive and to experience all that God has in store for you. Who would have thought that we would be alive to see the year Twenty Eighteen (2018) and the year 5778?

Are there promises that you are looking to be fulfilled in this **MEGA** Year? If so, review Chapter 6 and allow it to enlighten you with confirmation that whatsoever God has spoken it must be fulfilled. God is **NOT** a man that He should lie, nor does He change His mind. His yes is yes and His no is no. If He has open the door, no one can shut it and if He has closed the door, no one can open it. God has swung a door WIDE OPEN for you and it's like a garage door. It requires a numerical code to open the door and you have it. The key looks different from the any other key. That combination is 5778 or 2018 or both. Jesus is that Door and He's waiting for you to walk in so that you can experience the good life that's at hand.

A big part of living the life of Abundance is to understand times and seasons. They exist not by accident, but to be a guide for God's people to help them to understand when to go, when to pause, when to be still and when to activate. Life is so much more simple and peaceful when one knows what season of life he or she is in. He or she doesn't have to rush and speed up the process, because it's not possible. It starts and end when God says so.

God started a new season, a new era, a new year on September 21, 2017, called Rosh Hashanah. This is the Civilian Hebraic New Year, when it is said to be when God created Adam and Eve. It is a highly celebrated day by

Jews and non-Jews and should be one that is celebrated for all God's people. The Year 5778 is called Ayin Chet, which resembles the shape of a door. Again, this door is not a regular door that swings open and closes or even used by a regular key. This is like a garage door that only goes up in order to open. Its keypad is filled with numbers or if there's a pre-coded automatic remote for the door, it can be used to grant access. Since garage doors are bigger than regular doors, it looks like there's many **BIG** and great things in store you and me.

This is the **MEGA** Year, where God is Making Everything and Every-day in Him, Good Again. It's time to experience the BIG things. Stop playing small as God is a great Big God and He wants to give you great big things and a good life. God is removing any darkness from your life, so that you can experience His Light. It's time to speak "let there be light." It's time to declare your Wealth Transfer and your Palace TIME.

It's time to participate in the Awakening Strategy and stand on your Mountain of Influence. Are you called to occupy your space and activate your purpose to help Families? Are you called to the mountain of Education, Religion or Ministry, Government of Civic Duty, Arts & Entertainment, Business, Media, Healthcare, Science & Technology or Finance? This should be a very clear and specific answer. By now you should know where you believe you would be the most influential and where you have the grace to succeed.

One doesn't have to like the mountain to occupy it, in fact, the mountain you may be called to, it's a high probability that you don't like it at all, such as Government or Religion and really don't want to be a part of it. God is using that dislike so that you can be the difference-maker.

He's calling you to that sphere because you have seen things that you don't like and you want to change it. I don't necessarily like the MEDIA Mountain, because it's too political, very expensive, somewhat corrupt and doesn't really fit my personality. However, I know why God assigned me to that mountain and He's gracefully giving me strategies of how to navigate the Mountain.

It's time for God's people to stop fussing and arguing about what he or she doesn't like and do something about it. This is what the **MEGA** Year is about. It's time to **AWAKEN** the warrior within you. It's time to be all that God has called, chosen and created you to be and to do. The time is NOW!

## Benefits of Decreeing and Declaring

*"Thou shalt also decree a thing, and it shall be established unto thee: and the light shall shine upon thy way."*
***Job 22:27 KJV***

I believe that you are ready and fired up to be a difference maker and to decree and declare what thus says the Lord. One of the benefits that's outlined in this text, is that it has **78** declarations that you can use to decree and declare and activate the **MEGA** in your life. One of the questions I get asked, is how do I know what to decree and declare? What scriptures do I speak over my life? What are the right words to use to command my day that aligns with what God is doing and saying? Well, here are the answers. They are clearly written in this text for you. You can use these 78 declarations along with any other text in the word of God to decree over your life or situation.

As you prepare to audibly speak the **78** declarations or any other biblical decree, please know that there is a pre-requisite that must take place. To receive these benefits, you must first be a son or daughter of the Highest. One of the gifts of being a child of God is that you get complete access to **ALL** His Benefits.

According to Psalm 103:2-14,17-19,22 NIV *"Praise the Lord, my soul, and forget not all his benefits--- who forgives all your sins and heals all your diseases, who redeems your life from the pit and crowns you with love and compassion, who satisfies your desires with good things so that your youth is renewed like the eagle's. The Lord works righteousness and justice for all the oppressed. He made known his ways to Moses, his deeds to the people of Israel: The Lord is compassionate and gracious, slow to anger, abounding in love. He will not always accuse, nor will he harbor his anger forever; he does not treat us as our sins deserve or repay us according to our iniquities. For as high as the heavens are above the earth, so great is his love for those who fear him as far as the east is from the west, so far has he removed our transgressions from us. As a father has compassion on his children, so the Lord has compassion on those who fear him; for he knows how we are formed, he remembers that we are dust. But from everlasting to everlasting the Lord's love is with those who fear him, and his righteousness with their children's children---with those who keep his covenant and remember to obey his precepts. The Lord has established his throne in heaven, and his kingdom rules over all. Praise the Lord, all his works everywhere in his dominion. Praise the Lord, my soul."* When you belong to God you have access to all these benefits and more. He becomes your Healer, Provider, Lawyer, Protector and so much more.

Years ago, my father had prostate cancer and he underwent surgery to remove the cancer. For about two years everything was fine and it appeared that my dad was cured or in remission as some call in. Tragically the cancer came back or came back from hiding and this time it was more potent and powerful than the first time. His doctors pretty much said that there was nothing else they could do for him. He was just told to get regular checkups and hope that something changed. Thus, his disease became a death sentence.

One Sunday after I ministered at our church service, I extended an open invitation for salvation and to my surprise my dad came to the altar. Growing up, I never saw my dad attend church, but he always made sure that he sent us to church. The only time I saw him at a church service was at a funeral and even there, he hung outside the church. We grew up in Jamaica and it was mostly over 80 degrees so being outside was never a problem for him or anyone that wanted to be outside.

This Sunday something happened. I believed my dad was the last person that I prayed for. Prior to praying for him, I asked my dad if he was saved. I asked him if he had ever received Jesus Christ as his personal Lord and Savior. He had not, so then I asked him if he would like to be saved? Without hesitation, he said yes.

After my father accepted Jesus Christ as his savior, I did something I have never done before. I looked directly at my father and said, "it is illegal for two spirits to dwell in the same body, therefore I command the spirit of cancer to leave his body now, because the Holy Spirit now lives there." The following day was one of my dad's regular checkups for the cancer levels in his body. Long story short, to their amazing surprise there was **no cancer**.

There's nothing too hard for God and when you have accepted His Son it gives you direct access to receive all the benefits from Him. It's no different from places of employment. Upon being hired or even before, one of the things that's shared are benefits that comes with being a part of the organization. So, it is when you are in Christ Jesus, there are benefits that comes with being a part of the kingdom and the pre-requisite is your confession and receiving Jesus Christ as your personal Lord and Savior, like my dad.

Are you ready to live life fully every day? If you are not saved, have turned away from the faith, or just not sure, you now have the opportunity to be saved. If you are already saved, then congratulations, you have everything needed to Decree and Declare.

# Confession

It's a simple process that takes less than 5 minutes. It's a three-step process as easy as ABC!

1. Accept Jesus Christ as your Lord and Savior by saying out of your mouth that you accept the Lord as your Personal Savior.
2. Declare audibly that you believe in your heart that Jesus Christ died for you and that He is the risen savior that will return.
3. Confess your sins and ask him to forgive you and you should also forgive others that you need to forgive.

Congratulations! If you have just accepted Jesus Christ as your personal Lord & Savior, you can now fully participate in the blessings that are in store for you.

Date of Salvation: _____

# NOTES..........

## Journal the Journey

# 78 Decrees & Declarations

It is time to decree and declare. Start off by saying "This is the day that the Lord has made, we shall rejoice and be glad in it. Every good and perfect gift comes from God—therefore this year is both good and perfect because it comes from God!"

2018 is the MEGA Year. It's the Year of the Open Door, the year to decree, let there be light. It's the year of **LiFE**™ and the year of Abundance. It is a year when promises will be fulfilled, a year of goodness and one where many souls will be brought to the Kingdom of God. It's time for an awakening in your life and in the land.

A year of signs, miracles and wonders, a year of prosperity for the righteous ones, a year when God's people shall rule and reign and inherit the earth, by being owners and lenders, and never borrowers. A year of being debt free and drama free. **<u>BELIEVE IT & RECEIVE IT!</u>**

This is the **MEGA** Year when God is making any of these **MEGA's** be established in your life.

1. MAKING EVERYTHING GOOD AGAIN
2. Making Everything (Earth) Great Again
3. Making Everything in Great Abundance
4. Making Earth in Great Abundance
5. Making Exercising Good Again
6. Make Eating Good Again
7. Make Earnings Grow Again (Always)
8. Multiplying Every-day Good Again
9. Making Economy be in Great Abundance
10. Making Every Goal Achievable
11. Making ENTERTAINMENT Good Again
12. Making Employment in Great Abundance
13. Multiplying Earth's Good Economy
14. Making Entrepreneurship Grow Again
15. Making Everyone Give Again
16. Making Everyone Glad Again
17. Making Expectations Grand Again
18. Making Earth Godly Again

**I decree and declare that:**

1. This year 2018 is the MEGA Year and the Year to Make Everything Good Again. It's the Year of New Beginnings and the year of Manifestations, Elevation, Greatness and Abundance
2. This year of our lives will bring divine opportunities that WE will take full advantage of
3. This year is filled with wonderful surprises, supernatural breakthroughs, and miracles from Heaven
4. Today marks the end of a SAD (Standard Adult Day), depressing, discouraging past and the beginning of a prosperous, debt-free, disease-free, depression-free, happy future
5. God will grant us strategies for a prosperous and successful life
6. This year our Prayers will be answered SUDDENLY
7. We will Dance, Shout and Sing to the King
8. We will give more, because we HAVE MORE
9. Our minds will be filled with the knowledge of God's identity
10. We are empowered to accomplish that which we were born to do
11. You are all you were born to be

12. Every day of our lives is in sync with the perfect will of God
13. Our vision is clear
14. Our intentions are pure
15. His WILL BE DONE ON EARTH AS IT IS IN HEAVEN
16. Our relationships are healthy
17. Our minds are healthy
18. Our Finances Are Healthy
19. Our Faith is Healthy
20. Our God supplies all our needs according to His riches in glory

21. We live in a prosperous and healthy environment and we have GREAT NEIGHBORS
22. God has affirmed who we are
23. We are the light of the world and so we shall SHINE


**I decree and declare:**

24. Joy, peace, prosperity, and success belongs to us
25. We have healthy friendships and are connected to the right people
26. We are filled with Love for God and for each other
27. We have healthy family members

28. We shall use our gifts and they will make room for us
29. We have found FAVOR with God and with man
30. We walk in divine delegated authority and we are the head and not the tail
31. We are world changers and Kingdom Builders
32. We will live a legacy and leave a legacy
33. We have an inheritance from our Heavenly Father and we will leave an inheritance for our future generations.
34. We are renewed and revived
35. We walk in greatness and our brilliance radiates daily
36. We will GLORIFY the GREAT KING
37. We are creative beings and we will live a creative life
38. We are millionaires
39. We are Royalty and unique

**I decree and declare that:**

40. Our minds are healthy and strong
41. We have a CLEAR VISION of our Future
42. We have the Wisdom of Solomon to make wise choices
43. We will pursue and recover all
44. Restoration belongs to us

45. The blessings of the Lord are upon us and we are rich
46. WE are healthy in our minds, body, soul and spirit
47. We are VICTORIOUS
48. We will no longer STRUGGLE, but will THRIVE
49. OUR enemies are subdued
50. WE ARE fruitful in all OUR endeavors
51. WE have at least 7 streams of income
52. We are the head and not the tail
53. We walk in abundance and we have dominion over earth's economic system
54. We are DEBT FREE and are not slaves to anyone
55. Wealth is transferred into OUR hands, NOW, BELIEVE IT AND RECEIVE IT
56. OUR income will always be greater than OUR expenses
57. Christ already paid the PRICE and by HIS STRIPES WE ARE HEALED
58. WE HAVE AN ABUNDANCE OF money that WE need for day-to-day expenses
59. WE always have more than enough to give
60. WE will sow great seeds and we will reap even better seeds
61. WE joyfully give a tenth of all our earnings to God
62. There is no lack in our house, business or relationships

63. We finance God's people. The homeless, widow, orphans and the less fortunate are taken care of by us
64. OUR bank accounts are filled
65. OUR network and net worth increase daily
66. We have a great network and net worth

**I decree and declare that:**

67. WE are resourceful
68. Everything THAT WE need is available to US when needed
69. The DOORS ARE WIDE OPEN and no man can close it
70. WE will only speak and share the GOOD NEWS
71. WE will praise God in and out of season
72. OUR NEXT 7 YEARS ARE FILLED WITH ABUNDANCE
73. WE are transformed daily by renewing our minds
74. WE walk in the Supernatural and God's presence is always with us
75. Our SOUL is well
76. WE are loved and will show LOVE
77. This year is a good year
78. I decree and declare that you have stepped into your #**MEGA** Life and the #**MEGA** Cycle.

NOTES..........

## **Personal Prayer**

(Pray Out Loud)

Our Father which art in Heaven, Hallowed, Mighty, Great and Powerful is your Name. Let your Kingdom come and let your will be done in my life. Thank you for my daily bread… (the word). Forgive me for all my sins and debts as I forgive those that have sinned against me. Help me when I am tempted and save me from the evil one. For thine is the Kingdom the Power and the Glory, forever in Jesus Name!

Complete your personal prayer that's specific to you.

Dear God:

_____

_____

_____

_____

# Conclusion

*"When he had received the drink, Jesus said, "It is finished. With that, he bowed his head and gave up his spirit."*
**John 19:30 NIV**

Three (3) of the most powerful words that seals the deal in any area of life, are **"It is FINISHED."** When Jesus spoke that out of His mouth, He meant it. You are already pre-destined to finish what God placed in you. You were destined for greatness before the foundations of the world. It's not by coincidence why you are reading this book, it's by divine appointment.

It is time for you to truly walk out your **PURPOSE** and to live a life with meaning. You are alive for such a time as THIS! You can no longer run from the true authentic you. Proverbs

19:21 AMP reminds us that *"Many plans are in a man's mind, but it is the Lord's purpose for him that will stand"* and Romans 8:28 AMP *"We are assured and know that God being a partner in their labor all things work together and are fitting into a plan for good to and for those who love God and are called according to His design and purpose."* You are called according to HIS **PURPOSE**, so declare it and walk in it! YOUR TIME IS NOW!

Perhaps you have had some terrible years or maybe some great years. Perhaps you are going through a rough time right now, because there are still some fragments of the Reset that God is still ironing out. Perhaps you are fired up and ready to be the best you and to live the **MEGA LiFE**, but you're a little scared. Maybe you've had several ups and downs and have felt like giving up. No matter what state of life you are in, this is the Year of New Beginnings where

God is making all things new again. You have the opportunity to start all over again. God is patient, faithful, thoughtful, kind, loving, and should I say **patient** again and His will and thoughts towards you are good.

God does not desire to see any of His people perish and it's His will that you should succeed. This is the year to see with the mind and not with the physical eyes. It's the year of the Open Door and the year of New Beginnings. God is saying that this year **5778/2018** is the year of new beginnings, the year of the open door, the year of abundance, the year of life, the year of purpose and the **MEGA** Year, where He is personally **Making Everything Good Again** and **Making Every-day Good Again**. God saw that it was good when He created you, thus, you are His **good** creation.

NOTES..........

Whew! Pause! Take a moment and process all this MEGA Message. It's your moment to put your thoughts on paper. Journal the Journey.

_____

_____

_____

_____

_____

_____

_____

_____

_____

_____

## Appreciation

First, I thank God for giving me life, health and strength and the many gifts to be who I am today. I thank Him for His son Jesus Christ, my savior and to the Holy Spirit for being my guide. Thanks to the most wonderful man on Earth - my husband Kevel A. Anderson, Sr., who loves me with all his heart and gives me the space and time that I need to live out my purpose in life. To our beautiful daughters, Christina and Chassidy and our son A.J. and nephew (like a son), C.J. for their love, laughter and support. To my mom, Sharon and a host of family and friends, thank you! Thanks to the publishing team and the staff at Riley Press (www.RileyPress.com), and anyone who had anything to do with this book being released. Most of all thank you for investing your time and resources. Thank you for being a part of my life!

## About the Author

CAROLYN G. ANDERSON is the FRESH, dynamic and inspirational VOICE that's creating a buzz locally, nationally and internationally. She's a Talk Show Host, TV & Radio Personality, Keynote Speaker, Wealth Coach, Professor and the author of several books such as Living a Wealthy LiFE on Purpose, The 10 Laws of Authentic Leader-SHIP, Heal-thy LiFE-Heal-thy Land, Focus & Get Results, Pregnant with a

Promise, From the PIT to the PALACE and many more.

One of the nation's leading expert on the art of transformation, she is the Founder and Executive Vice President of Integrity Consulting and Coaching Enterprise (ICE), a corporate coaching, speaking and consulting firm with over 30 years of combined experience in strategic leadership, lean processes, six sigma, visioning, process improvement, coaching, contracting and negotiations, amongst other services.

A trained Army Soldier, Carolyn knows the discipline and FOCUS needed to hit the TARGET! She utilizes the same skills taught in the military to fight and WIN. She is a trusted voice and a ground-breaking Speaker-preneur. Amongst her many accomplishments and accolades, her all-time favorite role is being a mom and wife. Being a parent is a gift from God. She is purpose driven and lives life fully every day always walking in her divine calling.

She's an ordained Prophet and a Senior Leader of Kingdom LiFE Center, a global ministry. Learn more about her at www.carolynganderson.com or text DrCarolyn to 22828 to connect with her.

Be sure to share these hashtag **#The7Year, #MEGA, #MEGALIFE** as you are reading this book and as you begin to decree and declare what your seen (7) years of abundance will look like.

Join the Book Club **#DrCarolynBookClub** on Facebook Groups and let's stay connected. You can search for the book club and send us your request.

# Connect with us!

I would like to hear from you and your wonderful testimony from this book. You can email us at admin@carolynganderson.com or to join our Mailing List text DrCarolyn to 22828

Learn more about other products and services or for booking at **www.carolynganderson.com**

Like our Page
www.facebook.com/DrCarolynAnd

Follow us at: www.twitter.com/DrCarolynAnd

# Other Books by Dr. Carolyn

Pregnant with a Promise

Focus & Get Results

Heal-thy LiFE

Heal-thy Land

The MVP Year 2017

# New in 2018

## Heal-thy LiFE/Heal-thy Land 2<sup>nd</sup> Edition

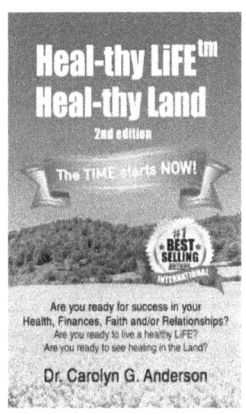

## The 10 Laws of Lead-er-SHIP

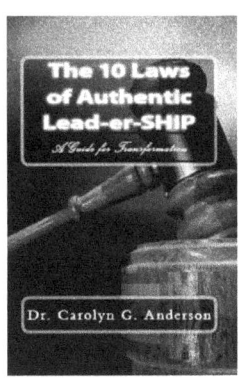

Living a Wealthy LiFE on Purpose

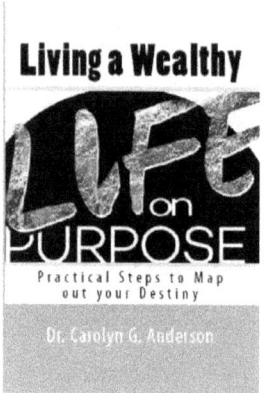

What Happens When the Dream Dies?

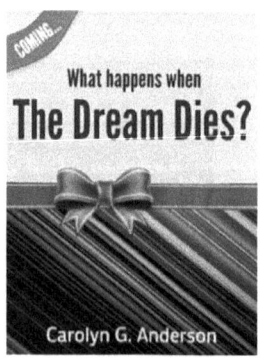

7 Steps to Break-through (Digital/Audio

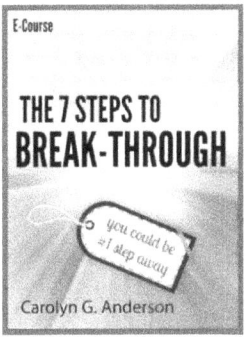

# Future Books

### #The7Year Series

**5779 - 2019 - Book 3**
**5780 - 2020 - Book 4**
**5781 - 2021 - Book 5**
**5782 - 2022 - Book 6**
**5783 - 2023 - Book 7**

www.ingramcontent.com/pod-product-compliance
Lightning Source LLC
Chambersburg PA
CBHW071156160426
43196CB00011B/2101